Winning the I.T. Project Management Job Interview

by Kuebiko Global

Contents

Acknowledgements...................................3

A Letter to the Reader............................4

1. Fundamentals of Interviewing...........9

1.1 The Interview Process...................................9
1.2 Common concerns of Candidates.................12

2. General Introductory Questions........15

3. A day in the Life of a PM....................38

4. Initiating a Project............................79

5. Planning and Estimating...................92

6. Project Execution............................120

7. Project Monitoring & Controlling....155

8. Project Closing.................................183

9. Management Reporting...................189

10. PM- Related Software Tools.............192

11. Application Development Management & DevOps...197

12. Agile Project Management...............211

13. People Management & Leadership..227

14. Dissecting Projects on your Résumé..241

Acknowledgments

We could not have written this book without the encouragement of students and teachers who pushed us to give our best. We were lucky to have incredible trainers (who are also senior industry professionals) who were instrumental in compiling this body of knowledge. Thanks to the hundreds of students we have taught over so many years that helped us by sharing feedback on their interview experiences. We also acknowledge and appreciate the role that our clients, families, and friends played in making this book a reality.

But our deepest gratitude goes to readers like you for purchasing this book. Thank you. We at Kuebiko Global wish you a happy journey and a very successful career as an I.T. Project Manager.

A Letter to the Reader

Dear friend,

This book is intended to help you in many ways. However, the fundamental objective is very simple – to help job seekers clear the interview process and land a job as an I.T. project manager.

There are many layers to this publication, and there is no unique author. This book is the equivalent of being able to sit one-on-one and pick the brains of dozens of senior industry professionals and hiring managers, and pack that knowledge into easily absorbed content. Don't read this book only once. Leave it on your computer and re-read it from time to time, especially before you put yourself out there in the job market (this includes seeking internal promotions and transfers, as well as applying to new companies). Even hiring managers can benefit from this book if they want to standardize or fine tune their hiring process and maintain question banks for their teams.

Kuebiko Global (www.kuebikoglobal.com) offers a variety of online training and interview preparation packages. Having been in this business for several years, we know that the interview process can be a very intimidating experience for job seekers. Often the students are disadvantaged, as there are not many resources out there that provide a practical, concise approach to learning how to clear interviews. As a result, many job seekers resort either to creating their own study materials from disjointed websites, or taking a best guess based on their academic training. However, the real world is an entirely different beast than what the textbooks present. This information gap provided the impetus for Kuebiko to compile a practical handbook of actual interview questions that will give job seekers the tools they need to succeed.

As professional trainers, we have access to hiring managers who are conducting I.T. project manager interviews on a daily basis and constantly improvising their approach to gauging candidates' knowledge in the shortest amount of time. Our trainers also work as industry professionals and cumulatively have conducted hundreds of such interviews. This book is a manifestation of these everyday interview experiences, so it's as real as it gets.

That being said, we also want to be transparent. We make no claims to have covered every possible interview question in this book. That would be impossible. Interviewers have their own approaches to conducting interviews; hence, a given question may be asked multiple ways by different interviewers. The intent of the questions and answers presented here is to serve as a broad superset of guidelines for what to expect in an interview. Additionally, each candidate should customize these answers to suit the projects described on their respective résumés, and not merely regurgitate the exact words written here. Each interview is about gauging how compatible your skill set is with the requirements of the job. To this end, the interviewer will probe your past experience and will attempt to link it to the skill set required for the job. Before stepping into any interview, you should understand the requirements of the position thoroughly, and should customize the answers found in this book to project yourself as the best fit for the job. Always breathe life into the interview by elaborating on your responses with specific examples from your résumé and work experience.

In addition to traditional questions, an interviewer may pose hypothetical scenarios, ask you to present material, create a high-level project plan on a whiteboard, or provide a high-level view of your past projects. Those are things that cannot be covered in a book.

Remember that an average interviewer rarely has more than one hour to speak with each candidate. All hiring decisions, either based on the actual answers or the manager's heuristics, are made early on, or within one hour at the most. That is why we have kept the book simplistic and minimalistic. It's like a real interview where you have around 2-3 minutes to speak at any given time. There might be a lot more information you could present in response to a question, but your speaking time is typically restricted to 3 minutes. Furthermore, interviews proceed with an assumption that your résumé accurately reflects your experience. You are not asked basic subject knowledge questions in an interview, and it usually starts from direct references to your past projects. Hence, this book is not a reference manual where we present flow charts and diagrams to break down and explain the subject of the question. The aim here is strictly interview preparation, and the assumption is that the reader has already trained or worked as an I.T. project manager and has access to some form of study material. Thus, we have made the answers as realistic as possible and have not provided extraneous subject-matter training material.

After going through these questions and answers, you can test yourself by having a friend ask you a few at random, or you can avail of our interview simulation package where one of our trainers can simulate a real interview for you and provide recordings. Whatever route you decide to take, ensure that the answers to the questions listed here are internalized and not merely memorized.

Thanks, and good luck with landing the job that you so deserve. We are here to help you at every step, so please feel free to drop us an email with any questions at info@kuebikoglobal.com.

Best wishes,
The Kuebiko Global team

1. Fundamentals of Interviewing

1.1 The Interview Process

Before we get into specific interview questions and answers for an I.T. project manager position, let us delve briefly into the FUNDAMENTALS of a typical interview process. The assumption is that you understand the hiring process and already have a good résumé in place. For additional information, you can log on to our website (www.kuebikoglobal.com) where you will find a webinar about hiring and interview processes, as well as résumé packs available for download. Let's cut to the chase and assume that you have already created a good résumé and are actively seeking on job sites and career portals.

If your résumé is shortlisted, then the first round is usually a telephone screening with the recruiter. The focus at this stage is high-level communication and evaluating how well you can articulate your key skills. It's essential to do well in the initial screening, as recruiters have the power to present you to the hiring manager.

The next round is usually a 30-minute to 1-hour telephone conversation with the hiring manager, and sometimes his/her colleagues. It is becoming more common now to use video conferencing software, as everyone likes to put a face to a name.

'In-person interviews' typically last up to a full day and involve meeting with several people. Be prepared to get repetitive questions, as not all companies are efficient, and different people may end up asking you the same types of questions.

Each interviewer will always start with an introduction to break the ice and will ask you to give an overview of your career trajectory.

Next, you will explain your role and the specifics of your latest projects. You will typically focus on your 2-3 most recent projects.

After this, the interviewer will delve into practical questions, asking how you would deal with specific scenarios. This part might involve some whiteboarding, and you may be asked for your opinion on different approaches in the project lifecycle.

Finally, they will close by evaluating your ethics, your career aspirations, and your level of interest in the job offered. The final question is typically, "Do you have any questions for me?" This is your chance to really get to know the job profile and the expectations. Do ask intelligent questions here, as this is an opportunity to both showcase your interest in the position and gather more information so you know exactly what you are getting into.

The picture below provides a visual representation of what to expect after the first round with the recruiter and a second telephonic round with the hiring manager.

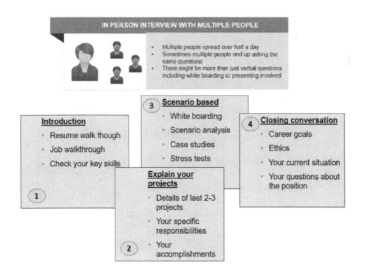

1.2 Common Concerns of Candidates

The following are some common concerns that people have about interviews for techno-functional roles like software quality assurance, business systems analysis, project management, and technology recruitment:

Will they ask me random questions on business domain?

No one asks too many questions on technical or domain knowledge outside what you have claimed on your résumé. Business domain and technology are very broad topics and your interviewer might not know a lot beyond their own area of work. However, certain jobs require expertise in a specific business area. For example, there are many jobs that will explicitly point out that they need someone experienced in investment banking, telecommunications billing, trade cycles, or a specific regulation in healthcare or financial services. In such job descriptions, the company will identify prior experience in that specific business process that is necessary for the job. So, if your résumé explicitly states that you have the requested experience, you may be asked detailed questions about it.

Will they ask me random questions about the dozens of software tools?

Unlike for programmers, tools are a means to an end for business analysts and project managers. It's not the end itself. There are way too many tools in the market and all of them are user-friendly with short learning curves. Thus, requirement management or project management software tools will never be the focus of the interview.

Will there be long, vague, certification-style questions?

No. The objective of a job interview is to find out whether you are a good fit for the job being offered. This is very different from obtaining an academic or professional certification.

Will they ask me to name my team members or provide the address of my office?

No, there will not be trick questions used to

determine whether you are misrepresenting yourself. The interviewer implicitly trusts you. However, before final offer, background checks are done by third party companies (not by the interviewer or the company itself) to check for red flags or criminal records.

Interviews are meant to evaluate whether you are a good fit for the team and can do the job. They are not like a college exam where all the material covered in your giant textbook is fair game. So, prepare efficiently. Do not try to cram in everything at the last minute. Understand the job requirements thoroughly and carefully prepare based upon the skills and requirements listed in the job description.

2. General Introductory Questions

1) Why did you choose I.T project management as a profession?

Answer: There cannot be one specific answer to this question. You will have to provide a brief background of your career trajectory so far. The main traits of an I.T. project manager are the ability to organize tasks, a thorough understanding of the software development life cycle, an understanding of people management, excellent communication skills, and ownership of high visibility projects from end to end.

If you started as a software developer, you can make a case of how you are well versed in different elements of technology architecture, which is beneficial to managing I.T. projects. If you do not have a software programming background, then you will have to explain how you got into information technology (possibly as a business systems analyst or a software quality tester) first.

From there, you need to explain why you wanted to move to the next level, which was being responsible not just for one aspect of the development lifecycle, but for the entire project. Explain that business cases, cost budgeting, general oversight, leading people, and driving projects to a successful closure were things that you did well and love to do. If you do not have a technology background, then you might also want to specifically mention that this is not a handicap because you have learned about the building blocks of technology and gained a thorough understanding of the software development lifecycle through years of working in the I.T industry. Also, explain how the lack of hands-on programming is not a handicap, as project management is not a programming role, but rather focuses on relationships, people management, and organizational leadership.

2) Describe your latest project with a very clear big picture.

Answer: *The following is strictly an example taken from a student's explanation of a project on his resume. You need to prepare something similar for at least the latest two projects on your resume. In an in-person interview, expect the interviewer to* *ask you to draw something on the board (e.g. high-level architecture) for the latest project. - KG*

Problem: Fannie Mae was handling and restructuring millions of dollars' worth of loans each minute but the systems they used were homemade excel reporting tools. This was initially managed by a huge team of loan processing analysts who used to manually update every single loan details and restructure them which resulted in inefficiencies mainly slow processing time, which was the result of the loan processing team updating and restructuring loans, periodic reporting since the team reported every month end and inaccuracies due to manual reporting.

Objective: The leadership wanted us to build an OBIEE system that would:

- Automate the process of restructuring delinquent loans to reduce the number of foreclosures that we were going through and align the process with regulatory standards like HUD Hamp guidelines.
- Report key mortgage metrics on a constant daily basis like mortgage installments,

balance, modified interest rate and term of the loan, and LPI dates. This system offered significant benefits like automation of millions of mortgage reporting and restructuring data, reducing processing time, and improving data accuracy.

Actions I took: I was hired at the start of the project and was fortunate to be involved in the entire lifecycle. My duties included, but were not limited to: floating an RFP, selecting the right vendor, building the initial team of business analysts, onboarding the vendor, creating a high level and low level project plan, controlling and monitoring the project through its entire lifecycle, managing customer expectations, working with the team during highs and lows, and closing out the project. I thoroughly enjoyed working on this project, and am very proud of its success.

Challenges: There were many challenges, some of which are listed below.

- The company was initially hesitant to allocate the budget that we required, and we had to work on a reduced budget.

- This was one of the strategic endeavors that had been promised to senior management, so there was extremely high visibility for it.
- The skill set required for working on the technical architecture proposed was not very common, so it was challenging to find the right resources.
- The functionality of the system was very complex, so it was tough to find qualified business systems analysts who were able to come up to speed fast enough to add value to the project.
- The clients were very demanding and would not be happy with anything less than perfection on the product feature. It was very challenging to work with clients who focus on such granular details.
- The quality of the initial build was not up to the mark as per client expectations, so we had to manage a lot of change requests very quickly and work at a greatly accelerated pace for the last 6 months.

Results: Our initial estimate for this project was 2 million dollars and 1.5 years. It did end up taking 3 more months, but we completed it under budget. Most importantly, the clients were very happy with the product we delivered. To this day, we are receiving accolades for its usability, how much time it saves, etc. which ultimately has a positive impact on the company's bottom line.

3) What are some things that excite you about your job?

<u>Answer</u>: There are several things I do every day at work that challenge me and keep me interested. Some of them are:

- Improve products by thinking about them from customers' perspectives
- Control large, critical projects where I get to be involved in every aspect of execution
- Learn new business domains and different business applications
- Learn how to manage different types of people at different levels
- Interact with business users to understand how their minds work and how they typically use products

- Interact with the technology team and business analysts to understand how to motivate and drive them

4) Please give me your opinion on the following statement: "A project manager is as good or as bad as his/her business domain knowledge or technology knowledge."

Answer: You need to answer this one based on the job requirements. If the position you are interviewing for clearly states that they need someone who has actually worked in a specific domain, then you cannot undermine the value of domain knowledge or hands-on experience by giving an opposite answer. That will surely jeopardize your chances of getting the position at the very onset of the interview.

However, if domain knowledge was not mentioned in the requirements, then you can infer that its importance depends on the type of project. In general, amongst the various techno functional roles, project management is the role that is the least domain-centric. Project management is a generic and transferable skill and does not require you to be very close to the business operation or domain. You can say that project management is a set of generic skills such as time management, people management, software development life cycle management, and quality management. It involves a lot of strategic planning, quick thinking, effective communication, and people skills. These are not related to business domain and technology, as there are other people on the project (e.g. business analyst or technology architect) who are responsible for managing those aspects.

However, it's always useful to gain domain knowledge in the project that you are working on for many reasons.

First, domain knowledge gives you a better quality of engagement with clients. Second, it helps you to put yourself in the client's shoes as you consider how to improve the product. Third, it can help you gain the respect of your team by coming across as someone who clearly knows what they are talking about. For these reasons, it is always good to understand the business operations of the project you are working on, but it is not always necessary to have expertise in it before the project starts.

5) If you were hiring a project manager, which traits would be most important to you in a candidate?

Answer: The primary traits that a project manager must have are as follows:

- Excellent communication skills
  - Ability to interact effectively with various stakeholders, team members, sponsors, vendors, customers, etc.
  - Ability to identify stakeholders, understand their needs and expectations, develop stakeholder engagement plans, and improve overall acceptance of program objective
- Experience managing all stages of the SDLC, preferably for both waterfall and Agile style projects
- A fair understanding of a developer's responsibilities and the various development best practices that are adhered to in big companies

- Excellent organization skills and ability to intelligently break tasks down to a manageable level
- Maturity in interacting with people and managing teams
- Understanding of typical challenges that different types of projects face and knowledge and experience in handling them
- Experience in management reporting and proactively identifying risks and potential issues
- Well-honed leadership skills in order to lead the program management team

6) If you were to change a few things about how your previous company functioned what would it be?

Answer: *You need to be careful with this one, as you cannot be too negative about a past employer or a past manager. Even if you want to point out some flaws, keep it very polite and be sure to also mention some positive things. You want to convey the flaws not as negative experiences, but as opportunities for improvement. -KG*

I loved the work environment of my previous company. Still, I think a few areas for improvement would be:

- Moving more projects to agile style methodology
- More automation in management reporting, as manual tasks consume lot of time and cause human errors
- Changing the way business cases are analyzed in order to understand project priority
- More standardization between different project teams for best practices, tools, PM processes, etc.

7) **Where do you see your career going in the short-term (3-5 years) and the long-term (7+ years)?**

Answer: *The answer to this really depends on your interests and the stage of career you are in at this point in time. Use the following career path as a guideline:*

Experience level 0-6 years:

Mid-level project manager – Handling projects of around 10-15 people (i.e. approx. $1.5 million budgets)

Experience level 6-12 years:

Senior project manager or program manager – Managing projects of 30-40 people (i.e. approx. $10 million+ budgets)

Experience level 12+ years:

Director or above – Managing portfolios of entire areas (i.e. approx. $20 million+ budgets)

8) Are you a team player or a lone wolf?

Answer: As a project manager, one cannot be a lone wolf. Project management revolves entirely around being a team player. It involves continuously communicating up and down, talking to team members to understand the status, proactively analyzing risk by holding team meetings, motivating people during difficult circumstances, etc.

There are very few tasks that one can complete as a lone wolf in project management. Some that do exist include analyzing the status, preparing management reports, and calculating cost plans. However, these are a small portion of the job, and the majority of it requires one to be a team player.

9) Do you like working in small teams or big teams

Answer: I have had a chance to work in teams as big as 40 people, and also in small teams of 3 to 4. While each situation has its pros and cons, I feel comfortable and work well either way.

For example, with a big team, you have more resources and a better division of labor. However, the coordination is challenging and chaotic.

Similarly, small teams can be nimble and are suitable for agile style development. However, the scope must be limited because of team size, and often the staff is stretched thin and must work longer hours.

10) Have you worked under pressure?

Answer: I am no stranger to working under pressure, and I tend to perform well even under serious time and resource constraints. Even when situations are dire, I am careful not to react impulsively or emotionally and to remain professional at all times. However, if I notice that the constraints might harm the team or the project, then I prefer talking with my manager about providing additional help in terms of time or resources.

For example, in my recent project, there was a situation that resulted from a tight timeline. The entire QA effort for the release of a very visible and significant application was expected to be conducted in just 2 months. This put a lot of pressure on the entire team, including myself. We had to put in long hours and come in on weekends. The project management strategy had to be extremely efficient to make sure that the entire gamut of user stories was tested in that time frame. I ensured that there was a lot of thought put into the plan before we actually started executing the tasks. Ultimately, despite all the challenges, we delivered the results and ensured that the project was completed in the stipulated time period.

11) Why should we hire you?

Answer: *This is a very common question in most interviews, including project management. The* *interviewer wants to gauge how confident you are about being a good fit for the job.*

You should mention your experience/background and how it pertains to the position. You can also mention your potential and your ability to succeed in challenging roles, as well as emphasize that the role in question seems to be just what you're seeking. You want to emphasize both your confidence and your demonstrated merits. - KG

Example: I know that with my diversified experience and knowledge of the project management process, I would contribute immensely to the success of the project. I am also extremely interested in this kind of role, which is an exact match for my skills and experience.

This is the generic message you want to convey, but in order to establish a perfect synergy and fit, you need to highly customize your answer using items on your résumé that correspond with the skills that they are seeking. -KG

12) Why are you looking for a change now?

Answer: *There can be many answers to this question based on your personal situation. The objective is to give a perception that the reason you are looking for a change is more than just a paycheck. Also, try to connect it with the key skills required by the job being offered. Never ever say you are looking for a change because of negative aspects of your current employer (e.g. low pay, bad manager, less work, or bad culture). Even if one or more of these things truly are the motivation, you should never mention this in an interview. We have provided answers for the most common scenarios below. -KG*

If you are a consultant:

We are at a stage where the project is in a steady state. We've returned more to a 'business as usual' operation with minimal new builds. As mine was a contract position, the need for a full-time PM is likely to end soon. This is why I am looking for a new project where I can add value to the organization while growing professionally. Your position instantly caught my eye because you are looking for someone who is well versed in turnkey projects, from vendor selection to closing. My last three projects have been full life cycle projects, so I think there is a great synergy here. My skills could really add value to your project.

If you are in a full-time job:
I have worked at my present employer for X number of years, and it has been a great journey. I still love my job and am very good at it. However, I have hit a ceiling in terms of development here, and I am looking for an opportunity to face new challenges, achieve certain key career aspirations, and grow within the industry. When I read your job description, it immediately piqued my interest as it seems like a perfect match for my skills, and a great opportunity to add value to your organization.

We have left the skill part generic in the answer, but make sure that you put the specific skill that the employer is looking for in the actual answer that you provide in the interview. -KG

13) What is your biggest weakness?

Answer: *You need to be very careful with this question. The temptation might be to say that you don't have any weaknesses, but this is never the right answer; we all have weaknesses. The weaknesses should be very vague and masked as potential strengths. Never ever state any of the job requirements as your weakness. Some examples are provided below, but you will need to customize everything for yourself. -KG*

- I am sometimes not as patient as I should be. In these instances, I try to take a step back and see if there is anything I can be doing to expedite things, as well as lend encouragement to the team.
- I sometimes let myself delve too deeply into the details, and later realize it wasn't necessary for the success of the project.
- Sometimes I feel like my work/life balance is lacking. I enjoy my work so much that I sometimes spend more time working than what many would find agreeable. I guess this goes along with the adage that if you do something you love, you'll never work a day in

your life. Still, this is an area in which I could improve.

- I like to ensure my work is of superior quality, but occasionally I feel like I am overly critical of myself.

- On occasion, I have been too tough with my team for not achieving perfection. However, as I've grown professionally, I've learned to channel that frustration into encouragement and motivation, actively seeking ways to expedite processes and ensure that each team member has what they need to fulfill their responsibilities.

14) What do you know about our company?

Answer: Whenever you are appearing for any interview, make sure that you have taken the time to review basic information about the company (e.g. company history, headquarters, employee strength, domain expertise, recent achievements, etc.).

There are two reasons that interviewers ask this question:

- To gauge your interest level in the job and the company. They're looking to see how well you have attempted to understand the job requirements and the company as a whole.
- To evaluate your knowledge and curiosity about the industry in general.

Do some research on both the specific position and the company in general so you can go in prepared for this questiton. If possible, look at the company's blog and find a recent achievement or press release that interests you; then let them know that this caught your attention, and ask a little more about it.

15) Tell me about a project that was not a success. What did you learn from that project?

Answer: *The wrong answer is to say that every one of your projects was a success. Describe any project in which you did not meet the targeted deadline, the budget, or missed the scope. We all have at least one in our past. Again, be able to tell this story in an organized and succinct fashion within 3 to 4 minutes. The second part is most important: what did you learn? You see, we learn* *the most from the projects that go wrong. Have a good lesson that you learned that you will be able to carry with you for the rest of your career to prevent that problem from occurring again. - KG*

Example: A few years ago, when I first started as a project manager, I got involved with a project that had extremely tight deadlines. In the middle of the project, I realized that the code quality of the vendor was subpar and certain activities critical to the project were lagging. However, the vendor engagement manager kept convincing me that he was on top of things and that the issue would be resolved by adding more people. If I had been more experienced then, I would have known that certain things cannot be achieved by just adding more people. An in-depth root-cause analysis and planning is required.

Additionally, I did not realize the importance of communicating early. I was confident that senior management need not be bothered with an 'Amber' rating and that we would internally take care of the situation. I was too focused on delivering the functional requirements to 100% that I overlooked the importance of non-functional requirements like performance and stability. Both decisions were incorrect in hindsight.

Unfortunately, by the time we communicated to management that the project was red, it was a little late. Fortunately, we were still able to salvage it by some creative workaround and long hours. We missed our deadlines, but by re-planning, we were able to deliver the project with a good quality product some 4 months later. I learned my lessons well and have applied them to all the projects that I have executed ever since.

16) If I were to contact your former employer, what would (s)he say about your decision-making abilities?

Answer: My ex-employer and my manager would say that I was a calm, logical, dependable, and methodical decision maker with great cost benefit analysis skills. They would also say that I had great people skills and instinct for predicting.

17) Do you have any questions for us?

Answer: *This is usually the last question of any interview. Make sure that you ask a few intelligent* *questions here, but always avoid asking about salary or benefits. Questions for the interviewer demonstrate engagement throughout the interview, as well as genuine interest in the job. Like many other questions, this is highly specific to the job that you are interviewing for, but here are some generic questions you can ask if they have not already been covered during the interview:*

- What type of project will I be managing?
- Has the project already started?
- Has the duration or budget been established?
- Who will I be working directly for (boss in the company)?
- Who is the client I will be working for?
- Do you have a "career growth path" for project managers?
- After we complete this project, what will I do next?

3. A Day in the Life of a PM

1) What is a project? How does it differ from a program? Can a project ever be a program?

Answer: A Project is a single endeavor with a start date, an end date, and a well-defined business goal. Programs are collections of projects, typically connected in some way. Projects within a program, if executed independently, do not give the desired business value. Hence, they are executed under a program.

Example:

A telecom company decided to launch its high-speed network. For this, they need to:

- Set up towers
- Install cabling and networking
- Advertise and market the new network
- Make updates to their portals for the new product

These 4 smaller projects could be executed together within a program called Launching High-speed Network.

Note: Sometimes a project is so big that it is considered a program because it would be too difficult to track at the project level.

2) If you are working as a project manager in an organization which is less mature in management terms and standards, what do you think would be the biggest challenges for you? How would you overcome these challenges?

Answer:

Challenge 1: Implementing PM best practices in an environment where its use and importance is understood only vaguely.

Solution 1: Forming a PMO within the organization establishes a specific group that will provide definition to PM best practices and it won't remain vague anymore. The type of PMO (weak or strong PMO) and its operating area (supporting / controlling or directing PMO) you would be implementing are a couple of things to consider before deciding the best route forward.

Challenge 2: Eliciting support from management for the PMO proposal & resistance to change.

Solution 2: I would use my negotiation skills with the people who resist changes, and would showcase operational challenges as future benefits. I would emphasize the benefits that the change offers, rather than focus on the short-term pain that change causes.

Challenge 3: The team members are hesitant to try out something unfamiliar.

Solution 3: I would start with baby steps and pilot projects for PM best practices, rather than go big bang. This way team members do not have to go all-in on new practices and operational models. Instead, they can start lean, then pick and choose what works along the way.

3) **You have been assigned as PM to a project which is running behind the schedule. What would your ideal approach be in this situation?**

Answer: I would be very careful and analyze the situation in depth before proposing solutions. On the face of it, additional resources would seem to be the answer. However, not all situations can be resolved by adding resources. In fact, the schedule can potentially be jeopardized by adding unskilled or unfit resources. Furthermore, adding resources can also cause the budget to balloon very quickly.

Therefore, the first option I would explore is whether a partial delivery is possible and if a minimum viable product can be worked out with the customer so that we get the application in production first. Additionally, I would analyze the bottlenecks and find the root causes of the delays. Once the root causes are established, we can begin to address them one by one. Some root causes that I have experienced in my career as a project manager are:

- Initial estimates were incorrect, and certain tasks were taking way more time than we initially expected.
  - In a situation like this, we need to be transparent and communicate to management that initial estimates were made based on information

available at that time and certain assumptions. We need to be clear on what assumptions did not turn out as expected and what information changed during execution. This should be used as a basis for a re-plan and a second, more accurate estimate

- External factors (e.g. dependency on operate teams, infrastructure teams, and red tape around certain processes) which could not have been foreseen.
  - o In these situations, we can bring the external factors to management's attention and request that they escalate or expedite
- Bad planning where critical paths have not been observed properly, or a lot of work falling on a few resources, resulting in an uneven distribution of work.
  - o In this situation, it is important to take a step back and be very specific in pointing out the exact resources that are overloaded or the critical paths that are holding up other processes.

- Constant requirement changes by the customer.
  - This is natural because typically clients come back with suggestions about product usability only after they have had a chance to see the actual product. No amount of wireframes or requirements elicitation can replace the experience of actually using the product.
  - However, it must be communicated to clients that it's not possible to accommodate everything they recommend post-signoff in the very first release. All feedback will be considered, but it must be a multi-step approach.
  - I would request the business analyst to maintain a proper log of which items are change requests and which are actual defects. The focus would be to remediate the defects first, and later provide a release schedule to the customers for enhancement requests.

4) What are the different types of organization? Which one gives the maximum power to the project manager?

Answer: The three different types of organization are as follows:

Functional organization: Where the functional manager calls the shots and project managers report to him/her;

Matrix organization: Where responsibility is split between functional and project managers; and

Projectized organization: Where the project manager has complete control over the project.

You can also mention weak and strong matrix as types of matrix organization.

As we know, projectized organization gives maximum authority to the PM. However, not all companies follow this. You need to ask the interviewer what type of organization they follow. Do not express judgment as to whether one type is better than another. There are pros and cons of each style of hierarchy, and you will need to work around whatever style management has decided is best for the organization. The important thing is to be familiar with each different type. - KG

5) As a PM in a matrixed organization, how do you go about getting things done?

Answer: In a matrixed organization, you do not directly manage the resources that work for you. This reduces the level of control you have over them. That makes it important to use either a guiding or delegating style of leadership, as an authoritative style will never work in matrixed reporting structures. One must take time to understand the team members' personalities, likes and dislikes, and what inspires them. Try to empower the team and avoid micromanaging. Give them an assignment and hold them accountable to their commitments. If ever there is a problem, take it to the responsible resource immediately. If you are not able to resolve the problem with that person, then escalate it to their manager.

6) You are working as a PM on a fixed cost project. Your organization is following

traditional waterfall method. You observe that your customer is changing requirements frequently, and this concern is raised by your team. How will you deal with it?

Answer: There are two ways to deal with this situation:

- Plan for partial delivery and convince the customer to incorporate change request delivery in another minor release. This would be a win-win situation.
- Plan for agile delivery with your management's cooperation. However, you need client participation for agile implementation. A client representative must work as Product owner and work closely with the team. Because this option has client dependency, it is less desirable than the previous option.

7) What are the different types of PMOs?

Answer: There are three types of PMO:

Supportive PMO: A supportive PMO is a centralized shared services organization. It typically will provide peripheral help, such as recommending best practices, providing project management templates, managing documentation in central share point sites, etc.

Controlling PMO: This PMO helps to reign in the activities (e.g. processes, procedures, documentation, etc.). Here, PMO conducts official reviews of the projects and guides the project team on following standard PM principles and guidelines.

Directive PMO: In this type of engagement, the PMO provides hands-on project management pertinent to the specific project. This can also include providing project management resources that work on different projects based on demand.

8) What is Organization Breakdown Structure (OBS)? Could you please explain the same with your present organization?

Answer: OBS is simply a hierarchical structure or model which describes the structure of an organizational framework for planning, resource management, time and expense/cost tracking, budget allocation, actual cost tracking, and work management.

For example, in my present organization, there are 6 program managers rolling into a director. I am one of the program managers. Each program has around 3-4 projects, each managed by a project manager. All the project managers report into a program manager. Each project manager has a team of 2-3 business systems analysts, 4-5 quality analysts, and anywhere from 10 to 20 developers depending on the size of the project.

While you are explaining the organizational structure of your organization, the interviewer is trying to determine where you stand in your organization and how your organization's reporting structure works. -KG

9) **You are working in an organization where the project team is not directly reporting to you. As a PM, you identified that one of the team members is always late to work, which**

is going to affect your delivery. How will you deal with this situation?

<u>Answer</u>: When a project team is not directly reporting to a PM, it's a matrix organization. In a matrix organization, resources report to functional managers and are assigned to a project which you, as a PM, manage.

In this situation, I would first talk with the team member to understand whether there is any genuine reason for the persistent tardiness. The intention would be to find out if there is anything that I can do to provide an amicable solution to the problem.

If the reason for the tardiness is genuine (e.g. dropping a child off at school, taking a spouse for physical therapy appointments, etc.), I would offer help by providing the option to work in different time slot or work from home (Note: this option varies from organization to organization, so I would seek the resource's manager's approval before offering any accommodation).

However, if I found the reason was not valid, yet continued to occur even after a discussion, I would approach his/her functional manager for input on how to proceed and assistance with same.

10) Your supervisor has directed you to implement something you do not think will be helpful. How will you convince your supervisor that the idea should not be implemented?

Answer: I would never directly object to the idea provided by my manager, or anyone else for that matter, without first thinking through it thoroughly. However, if I was unable – even after careful consideration - to see the value in an idea offered by my manager, I would step up and ask the manager for a more detailed explanation as to why (s)he backs the idea. After said explanation was given, I would ask any questions I might have. This process would be to ensure that I had considered all perspectives.

If I was convinced that I had not missed anything, and knew that the idea would be detrimental, I would then determine how best to present my opposition. I would list out the pros and cons of proceeding with implementation, using examples from my past experience to show why the possibility of the idea working out is bleak. Additionally, I would make it very clear to my manager that I am doing what I think is in his/her best interest to try and avoid a decision that we may regret later. This way the opposition is impersonal and is presented as a means of supporting the manager.

11) What is a milestone? Explain with an example.

Answer: A milestone is a kind of task in project management. It is used to mark specific points on the project timeline.

Examples: Project start, phase completion, customer signoff, project closure, etc.

12) What do you mean by customer-based Service Level Agreement (SLA)?

Answer: SLA is simply a contract where you define the service that you are going to deliver to your customer. It basically defines what the customer should expect and when (s)he should expect it. Customer-based SLA is a type of SLA documented for individual customers with all the services they use.

13) Please provide one example from a project where you did something new and explain the outcome.

Answer: *You should discuss something you did as an experiment and be honest about its outcome. If it worked out, that's great. If not, explain why it didn't work and indicate whether you tried the same experiment again to make it work.*

The interviewer is keen to know if you like to experiment and whether you believe in yourself. If you fail on the first attempt, do you try again?

A few examples of innovative things people have done in projects are listed below. You can use any of the points below and add your personal experience to make it more compelling. - KG

- Changing the development methodology from waterfall to Agile
- Trying out a new vendor for a project
- Automating the management reporting and PMO reporting

- Trying out a new role, like usability expert, which was not used previously
- Standardizing tools and SDLC process across the organization
- Trying out new tools for requirements analysis and project management to increase project efficiency
- Recommending QA automation

14) Please provide an example from a project where you found the situation very challenging and you had to accept assistance from your senior peers.

Answer: *The purpose of this question is to understand whether you are comfortable seeking help when required. An incorrect response is that you have never required help. You can start by saying that when you are not 100% certain of something, you are keen to learn from others. Below are some general examples/statements which you can draw from and add your specific experiences. -KG*

When you are new to a project it is sometimes difficult to understand the processes around acquiring software and hardware infrastructure. Seniors who have been in the organization longer can provide excellent insight. Some examples from my project are:

- In one of my early projects, I was not completely familiar with the process of RFPs or the underlying technology of PEGA BPM. I consulted with senior technology architects and a more experienced program manager who helped me with the process.

- When trying to resolve issues related to stability, performance, system security, and other such nonfunctional areas, I request help from various shared services groups, as I am not the expert in these areas.

- If my project is very data intensive, and I am struggling with managing the data aspect, then I seek help from senior members of the data management center of excellence.

15) Give one example where another project manager within your

organization approached you for suggestions/guidance and you helped them out with your advice.

Answer: Any specific example where you might have guided or helped your peers can be helpful. Some general examples are as follows:

- Helped another PM with MS project EVM report
- Helped a newly onboarded PM in updating the project calendar, as (s)he had not previously used MS project
- One of your PMs wanted to have a SharePoint site for his/her project but was not very familiar with SharePoint. You helped him/her in understanding the different uses for SharePoint and how it can be a valuable tool. You helped him/her with creating a SharePoint list and demonstrated how to add filters, conditions, etc.

Additionally, you can customize any of the points provided in the previous question. - KG

16) You are in a meeting with your team. You found that only senior members

of the team are active and new / junior members in the team are not opening up. How would you make them feel comfortable with the meeting environment?

Answer: This question aims to understand how you build a healthy and friendly environment within your team. The interviewer wants to know whether you are friendly enough with the team members and foster an environment where everyone feels comfortable during the meeting.

Examples:

- You introduce new team members during the meeting and ask other members to introduce themselves.
- You assign a buddy to each new resource joining your team so that (s)he gets used to the project environment.
- You touch base with new members and make them feel comfortable, ensuring they are provided with the necessary assets, accesses, tools, etc.

- You have a proper plan for knowledge transfer whereby you assign the knowledge transfer work to existing team members; after a few days, you plan for reverse knowledge transfer where the new member explains what all (s)he has learned.

- You pose specific questions to the new team members during the meeting to encourage their participation.

- You ask the new team members about their previous experience to see if they have suggestions for improvements or alternate approaches in your organization.

17) How do you differentiate whether something assigned to you is a project? If you have been assigned to maintenance work, how would you explain to your supervisor that it's not a project?

Answer: *This question seeks to understand how you define a project. A project is a temporary endeavor (it's not ongoing). It should have a purpose and an end date. - KG*

I would explain to my supervisor that because the assignment is more of a maintenance/operational nature, there is very little work for me to do. I would explain that the work is not technically a project, and that my skills will be underutilized there. I would never directly reject the proposition, as I don't want to give the impression that I only work if given specific types of assignments. Instead, I would present it in such a way that will help my supervisor understand that I'm willing to do something more challenging and want to contribute my maximum effort. It's not possible to contribute my maximum effort if I'm given assignments where my potential is underutilized.

18) What is your most time-consuming task in your project?

Answer: *Project managers spend the majority of their time on communication activities such as meetings, status reports, follow-ups, interviews, review meetings, etc. Planning and monitoring controlling activities are also very time-consuming for a PM.*

Your answer will be based on your own experience and the types of projects you are working on. Below are some general examples. - KG

- Follow-ups on tasks, dependencies, defects, feedbacks, signoffs, approvals, etc.
- Team meetings or status meetings with different stakeholders
- Project planning, understanding the risks, and preparing in-depth mitigation plans

19) Do you believe in delegation? How do you decide whether to delegate a task?

Answer: Yes, absolutely. Delegation is essential to a PM. It shows two things:

- You believe in your team
- You are providing your team members with opportunities to learn and grow

If you find the task or assignment can be done by someone within your team and (s)he is willing to take up new challenges, you can delegate it. However, your job does not end at delegation. Depending on the maturity and capability of the individual, regular follow-ups, guidance, and coaching may be required to ensure timely and quality completion of the task.

20) How important is the process implemented in your project? If a team is in favor of Agile methodology, but management wants a combination of waterfall and Agile, how should a PM reconcile the competing views?

Answer: This depends on each organization and its management. If your organization is following CMMI or any other process framework, it's mandatory for you - as a member of the organization - to follow the same. This is organization level initiative, and you can't resist it just because you or your team is not comfortable doing it.

The general industry understanding is: if you are working in Agile methodology, then it's very difficult to follow a process (especially the documents mandate that CMMI enforces). However, there are few organizations which are doing Agile. You can explain to your team that this is an organizational initiative, and is, therefore, non-negotiable. At the same time, you should keep your management informed about the challenges you and your team are facing.

Note that you can resist or raise your or your team's concerns to a certain level, but not beyond that. Sometimes you need to find a middle ground or workaround to organization-level mandates. There is a reason why some things are mandated; while you may find them frustrating at a tactical lever, it's entirely possible that they have long term or higher level benefits. So, it's best to find a middle ground in lieu of confrontation.

<u>Examples:</u>

- Management decides to use a shared services model for business analysis, production support, or quality assurance. This means that people working on your project will functionally report into a central organization and your control becomes a dotted line. Most managers would not prefer this for their projects, but it might make sense from an organizational standpoint. In this situation, a PM must find the best way to get the job done. This can include putting together quality assurance plans and processes so that you can hold the central team accountable for meeting your expectations.

- Your PMO might impose more layers of reporting for projects, and some of the reports might appear redundant. However, these reports may be a requirement to which management must adhere.

21) Please provide one example of a serious conflict you observed during a project and explain how you dealt with it.

Answer: This is a very standard question which should be expected in any managerial interview. Conflict is inevitable in a project environment, so you should draw from your previous project management experience to answer this question. Some examples include:

- In one of my projects where I was the program manager, there was a frequency mismatch between the project manager and the business systems analyst. This would lead to daily confrontations and lack of teamwork.

I spoke with each of the concerned members separately and understood that there were two issues. One was a direct personality clash and the other was that the BA wanted to be the PM because he felt he would do a better job of managing the project.

I explained to each of them that their issues were not only slowing down the project but also decreasing the morale of the rest of the team. I explained to them that we should not let our personal interests get in the way of doing our jobs and that we must treat the workplace in a professional manner. I segregated the duties and made it very clear what was expected from each of them. I also assured the BA that if he felt ready to be a PM, we could begin discussing his career path, but arguing publicly with the PM would not help earn him a promotion. Both understood the issue, and over time the situation improved greatly.

- On another project, there was an incumbent technology team lead who also used to double as a business analyst because she had become familiar with the business users and processes over the years of working there. However, we decided to hire a new dedicated business analyst, as the BA duties were taking too much time away from the tech team lead's main job of technology architecture. The team lead wound up feeling a loss of control and having too many conflicts with the BA down the line.

Upon further investigation, we also realized that the technology team had gotten used to directly dealing with users without any underlying documentation, so the introduction of a BA was perceived as a needless overhead that caused delays. I had lengthy conversations with the tech team to explain to them that they would under no circumstances lose control, but instead would be able to focus more on their jobs by letting a BA do the user interaction and requirement management. I explained the to the BA it's important to keep the technology architect in the loop for key requirements discussions, and how the constant feedback should be taken from the tech team to ensure that the documentation that is created helps them better understand the specifications and not delay their work. This approach worked well: the team went on to form a cohesive group and deliver many projects.

22) How frequently do you conduct your team meetings? What does a typical agenda entail? What are a few questions that you ensure you are putting on the table?

__Answer:__ This varies from project to project. In some projects, team meetings happen weekly or bi-weekly. Some PMs prefer to meet with their teams daily. You can provide your answer and the justification behind the frequency of the team meeting that you may have.

Team meeting agendas should focus only on the project. You also need to include other topics like organizational updates, project updates, feedback, any important communications, any updates in team structure, any product release or new joiner in the team, questions to your team members about their comfort level, etc.

23) Do you document minutes after each meeting? Do you follow up on the action points until closure?

Answer: This should always be a yes. As a PM, you should always be concerned about whether action points are getting tracked until closure. This has a direct impact on your project, and you should keep tracking all the action points from the meetings. Minutes of the meeting (MOMs) also help in documenting any important decisions or exchanges of information that might have happened during the meeting.

24) A contract manager is working on drafting a contract for your project. You have been asked to assist her. As a PM, you are aware that the project scope and deliverables are not very

clear. Which type of contract would you prefer and why?

Answer: I would prefer a cost plus fixed fee contract (CPFF). In cost plus fixed fee projects, the seller can exercise control over the cost, rather than get locked into a rate or a price. Note: in a project with limited scope clarity, incentives are hard to define and agree.

25) What are your key professional achievements, particularly in your career as a PM?

Answer: Make sure you are honest answering this question. It is not necessary to cite exceptional achievements which you feel will impress the interviewer. Any achievement or success that you feel was important for you will suffice.

Everyone has some project or professional experience that they hold close to their heart. You could discuss your favorite project, explaining why it was your favorite (e.g. you got to learn something new, got to interact with top management, had a chance to present in front of a large audience, etc.).

26) What is a Standard Operating Procedure (SOP)? What are the benefits of having SOPs?

Answer: This question should always be expected for senior positions.

These are the kinds of guidelines set by management, or the corresponding body in the organization, to guide employees in carrying out day-to-day operations. In software firms, SOPs are very important. This document guides the team on how to execute the project. The purpose of an SOP is to hold various parties accountable for their deliverables and define standards on what is acceptable and what is not.

Typical examples of standard operating procedures applicable for a project manager are:

- PMO can establish guidelines on which development methodology to follow for each type of project.
- PMO can establish standards and guidelines on required documentation for various phases of the project.

- PMO can establish standards for the milestones that will be used to track projects for different types of SDLCs. The granular plan and task breakdown is always the prerogative of a project manager, but the high-level milestones are typically set by PMO to enable efficient management reporting.
- There can be centralized guidelines on escalation procedures.
- The vendor management office can set up guidelines on vendor request for proposals (RFPs), selection criteria, and project type (i.e. fixed bid, investment project, time and material, etc.).

27) At what point do you find it necessary to bring others into your decision-making process? Why?

Answer: *This question is asked to understand the escalation mechanism you follow. Make sure that you are using words like **conflicts, communication management, RACI matrix,** etc. The interviewer is basically trying to judge both your PMP skills, as well as the way you involve* *others in the decision-making process. Be ready with an example. You can mention how you accepted input from junior team members, as well; doing so will demonstrate that you value all viable experience and input – not just that of the most experienced individuals.*

Examples:

- In any technology architecture decision, especially if one does not have hands-on knowledge;
- In key decisions, such as deciding the winner of an RFP process or negotiating a contract with a vendor;
- For any hiring decision
- For any urgent escalation of incidents, problems or major events disrupting service.

28) What is the difference between *assignment* and *delegation*?

Answer: An *assignment* is the process of transferring responsibility and accountability for a task from one person to another. *Delegation* is the process of transferring responsibility and authority for performing a task to another person. Assignment is generally a top-down approach, while delegation is more lateral and views a team member as a peer.

Assignment's only objective is to distribute work for completion. Delegation seeks not only to distribute work but also to instill confidence in team members and help them to realize their full potential by matching the work to the behavior and competencies of the delegated resource. Furthermore, delegation helps the resource to learn and grow by allowing him/her the authority to react to situations and make decisions.

29) Tell me about a time when you demonstrated leadership in a previous job.

Answer: This question expects you to give specific examples, if possible, or at least the generic way you improved your leadership skills in a previous role. The primary responsibility of a leader is to lead the team by mentoring and guiding toward the project goal. Don't forget to discuss how you accepted the responsibility for failure instead of placing that responsibility on any team member – even if they were ultimately at fault.

Be sure to include keywords such as lessons learned, OPA, etc.

Example:

I once inherited a team that was working on a very critical visible project that had faced many delays in the past. This was because the previous project manager had left the organization and a replacement was urgently required. I soon realized why other project managers who were familiar with that area did not want to touch the project. It was poorly managed and had already missed deadlines. I decided to resolve the situation without panicking.

The first step was to analyze the problems. The first problem was that there were no processes around requirements management and release management. It was too ad hoc and the people who had been working had gotten used to the ad hoc approach. They did not realize that the ad hoc method did not work and was causing chaos and missed deadlines. I set up a very specific process to requirements management, introduced documentation templates, and also introduced processes for Agile-based sprint management using a software called 'Rally'. There was a severe lack of communication in the team and people would rarely speak up even if they were aware of certain risks to the project. I set up regular communication sessions and one-on-ones which acted as safe zones for people so that they could communicate and escalate if they knew a potential risk. This helped us eventually get to a new project plan which had much more realistic timelines. We used that project plan to communicate to senior management about the actual reality and how we should face it, instead of falsely continuing to believe that the project would be done in 2 months and failing at the last minute.

Management appreciated the honesty and gave us permission to go ahead with new timelines. We were able to successfully execute the project and keep all stakeholders in the loop at every step of the way. Thus, I brought a struggling team together, implemented best practices, streamlined communication, and exhibited leadership by delivering a critical project.

30) As a project manager, what do you think is the biggest challenge any PM faces in his role?

Answer: *There are many challenges that any PM would face while managing a given project. You will almost certainly be asked a secondary question asking you to build on your answer by providing a personal example of the challenge you've described and explaining how you overcame said challenge. Some examples are provided below. You should make your answer very specific by customizing it to your projects. - KG*

- Requirements are constantly changing
- Resources are not available for a particular skillset
- Critical resource had an emergency during an important part of the project or left the company during an important phase
- Initial estimates were incorrect because of assumptions that did not play out as expected
- Coordination between onsite and offshore teams is challenging because of cultural differences

- Some resources on the team are underperforming and demotivated
- Management has mandated certain decisions that the team is not handling favorably
- Management has mandated certain processes that the team perceives as overhead and wasted time
- Sourcing hardware and software infrastructure is much more challenging than initially anticipated
- Customer is extremely demanding about the quality of the product
- Customer is unable to differentiate between a defect and a bug and is referring to all enhancements as defects
- Customer's prioritization is very different from what would have been preferable for technology

Again, for each of the challenging situations listed above, you must breathe life into it by using very specific examples. One example from a real project is shown below. You can use it to create similar examples for any of the situations listed above. - KG

Example: On one of the projects that I was leading, we were asked to implement an off-the-shelf enterprise project management software. Our client was very smart and had advanced through her career as a developer. She understood how to build software from the ground up, but this off-the-shelf software was proprietary, and the code could not be accessed through normal means. There were many tense meetings and conversations where she felt things should be easy or simple to adjust. We spent many hours calmly teaching and training to help her and her team understand how the software they had purchased actually worked. That project ended successfully, and the client was so pleased with both the product and the extra support provided by the team that she reached out to us for another project later on.

31) Describe a week in your life as a project manager while in the Execution phase of a project.

Answer: I like to conduct a very short daily standup meeting with my core team members early each morning. It is a quick "round-table" in which each person states a) what they worked on yesterday, b) what they plan to work on today, and c) any help needed.

During the Monday-Thursday meetings, I focus on ensuring that my team members are progressing on their planned activities. I work to resolve any issues identified or mitigate any risks.

I also like to establish weekly recurring status meetings, which I always try to schedule on a Friday. During the status meeting, we review the schedule to determine what was supposed to be completed. I then gather updates from the assigned resources as to whether the task was completed, and we update the schedule based upon their responses. Near the end of the meeting, we examine the schedule to determine what our targets should be the following week.

One of my final tasks each week is to prepare a weekly status report for my project stakeholders. This report has varied on almost every project I have managed, but the fundamentals are the same: How are we progressing with respect to the timing of our deliverables? How are we doing with respect to costs? Are there any issues for which we need help from management?,

32) What is the largest project you have managed with respect to budget?

Answer: *Know this answer well and be ready to back it up with data.*

As crazy as it sounds, there are project manager candidates who can't tell their interviewer about the budget for their project. If you are managing costs, you certainly should be familiar with the project's budget. If you are not managing costs, you are not a true project manager. For this question, a higher budget will clearly be more impressive to the interviewer and therefore score you more points. However, again, be thoroughly prepared to back up your answer with data. A smaller budget with ample data will always get you further than an answer you've fabricated or embellished in order to impress, but which you cannot support.

4. Initiating a Project

1) What kind of preparation should occur prior to initiating a project kickoff meeting (KOM)? Who would be participating in the KOM?

Answer: Pre-KOM preparations should include a detailed agenda for the meeting, invitations to all participants, project charter preparation and approval, and a slideshow covering the following:

- Project objective and high-level deliverables, project duration, and cost of the project
- Milestones and tentative delivery date
- Initial risk and mitigation plans
- Dependencies and open action points
- The best way forward and execution plan

KOM participants should include team members, project sponsor, and stakeholders (i.e. any other team or representative who would be affected by the outcome of your project).

2) You have been given an RFP, and the pre-sales team has asked you to assist them with the bill of material (BOM) and cost determination. You have noticed that the proposed quotes will result in a loss. Which part of the BOM will you try to reduce in order to increase return on investment (ROI) and make the project profitable?

<u>Answer:</u> The BOM is an itemized list of items for which the client must pay the expense. There are two components in a BOM - capital expenditure (i.e. one-time cost) and operational expenditure (recurring costs). In order to increase the ROI, you have to reduce operational expenditure.

3) You have been assigned as PM on a big budget project, and the sponsor has asked you to work on a project charter. What all will you include in your project charter? Who approves the project charter?

Answer: The project charter is approved by the project sponsor. It is typically a sponsor responsibility but is frequently delegated to the PM.

My project charter will include the following:

- Project objective/goal
- Stakeholders
- High-level scope
- Identified risks
- Expected benefits
- Estimated cost
- Expected timelines

4) Are you familiar with murder boards? Can you describe your experience using this concept in projects?

Answer: *(Note: There is also another name for murder board: "scrub-down." An interviewer may refer to it by either name or both.) - KG*

A murder board is a committee which critically reviews project proposal, questions why the project is being undertaken. If the murder board is not satisfied with the answers, the project is rejected.

The murder board – hence its name- ultimately decides whether the project 'lives' or 'dies'.

In most companies that I have worked for, murder board is carried out via the business case. There were in-house tools where I (as a PM) worked with management to enter all the details required to make a business case for a proposed project. This typically includes project details such as costs, timelines, business utility, urgency, people involved, and benefits both short- and long-term.

Initial funding is the first step. Then, depending on where we are in the project, there may be a second step and final round of funding. All of this must first go through the I.T. management team and finally be approved by the company's finance team. Finance and accounting will also provide guidelines as to which parts of the project can be *capitalized and which cannot.

*Capitalization occurs when expenses are not incurred in the accounting books immediately but are deferred to a future date. When we get to the future date, the expense can be amortized in installments.

5) What do we mean by *program roadmap?*

Answer: *This is a basic question if you are appearing for a program manager interview.*

A program roadmap is a chronological representation of the key milestones planned along the way for the project to be completed successfully. Program roadmaps also establish program activities and expected benefits, as well as depict dependencies between milestones. They can be used to show how different components are organized within major stages or blocks, and they illustrate how the capability is delivered through incremental releases.

You may also be asked why program roadmaps are important in program management. You should answer that program roadmaps are valuable tools for managing the execution of the program and assessing progress toward achieving the expected benefits. -KG

6) Who are different stakeholders in the programs that you manage?

Answer: This is a straightforward question. Examples include:

- Program sponsor
- Governance board
- Program manager
- Project manager
- Program and project team members
- Funding and performing organization
- PMO
- Customer and potential customer
- Suppliers

7) What are the main phases of the program lifecycle?

Answer: *This question, generally, is one of the first few questions asked in a program manager interview. The main phases are listed below. You may also be asked about the sub-phases for each main phase, so the sub-phases have been provided below as second-level bullets. - KG*

- Definition
  - Program formulation
  - Program preparation

- Benefits delivery
  - Component planning and authorization
  - Component oversight and integration
  - Transition and closure of the components
- Closure
- Mapping of program life cycle to supporting activities like production support and enhancement planning

8) As a program manager, you are very close to initiation. Which activities are included during the program initiation phase?

Answer: Program initiation is not a phase itself, but a sub-phase of the program definition phase. Typical initiation activities include:

- Program sponsor selection and financing
- Program manager assignment
- Scope, resource, and cost estimation
- Initial risk assessment
- Business case updates

- Program roadmap development
- Program charter development

9) What is *opportunity cost*? Provide an example.

Answer: Opportunity cost is the cost of a project, A, that you let go in order to choose another project, B. If you decide to go with project B, perhaps because it has a higher internal rate of return (IRR), then the cost of project A becomes an opportunity cost. You had a chance to gain the cost of project A, but you sacrificed that opportunity in favor of project B.

10) What is *business value*?

Answer: Business value is a concept that is unique to each organization. It is defined as the *entire value of the business* - the total sum of tangible and intangible elements. Tangible elements include monetary assets, fixtures, equity, utility, etc. Intangible elements could include brand recognition, public benefits, trademarks, etc.

Note: Although some organizations are not business driven, all organizations conduct business-related activities, and they focus on achieving the business value of their activities.

11) Are you familiar with the term *EVA* in terms of project selection? What does it stand for?

Answer: EVA stands for 'Economic value added' and is a term used in cost management. However, we also use EVA in project selection in order to determine whether a given project will provide the company with a return greater than its initiative costs.

Note: EVA, as used here, is unrelated to earned value analysis. Earned value analysis is a different concept where you evaluate a project's progress and forecasted completion by checking the cost till that point in time and the variances from what it should have ideally been.

12) When you set up a meeting, what ground rules do you follow?

Answer: *This is a simple question intended to evaluate how well you prepare for and conduct* *meetings. Below are some examples of ground rules, but you ought to elaborate a bit more using personal examples. - KG*

Examples:

- Set a time limit and keep to it
- Schedule recurring meetings in advance
- Ensure that each meeting has a well-defined purpose
- Stick to the agenda
- Bring the right people together and ensure each person is aware of his or her responsibility
- Document and publish the meeting minutes

13) How do you plan for a project?

Answer: I never do everything by myself. I try to find the right team members who are subject matter experts in the scope of what the project needs to achieve. I then collaborate with those individuals as a team. They come up with initial estimates, and I go over those estimates and questions as applicable. I draw upon each of their individual strengths, and -

perhaps more importantly- the strength of the team as a whole.

Once we have a basic plan in place, we decide whether the estimates are realistic and whether they are in alignment with management's expectations. Sometimes it can be a give-and-take exercise between the team and management deadlines. We then work to develop the series of actions or tasks that are necessary to move us from this idea to a completed project.

14) What are things that you have found to be low priority when planning for a project?

Answer: Most of the fundamental elements (e.g. scoping exercises, risk planning, communication planning, etc.) are always non-negotiable and high priority. However, it is counterproductive to overanalyze negative scenarios or waste too much time thinking about situations that have a low probability of occurring. I would consider planning for those unlikely and negative scenarios to be low priority until they actually occur.

15) What are the three constraints on a project?

Answer: The three primary constraints of a project are: Scope, Cost, and Time.

However, there is a fourth dimension that should be added as well: Quality.

I tend to think of Scope, Cost, and Time as being the legs of a three-legged table. If you adjust one leg, you must adjust the other legs too. The whole time you must keep an eye on that bowl of Quality sitting on top of the table so it doesn't spill!

16) You have just been handed a new project. Where do you begin?

Answer: The first step is to meet with my project sponsor. My project sponsor is my key to success. I say this for a few reasons:

- The project sponsor has insights about this project that I need to understand.
  - These insights will generally lead to success.

- The project sponsor can help me resolve problems if ever I get stuck.
- Finally, the project sponsor is generally a little higher within the management ranks of the organization and can help me navigate the political waters.

My next step would be to get to know the stakeholders and define two important things: high-level scope and success criteria. This sets the tone for everything that follows. I would then meet with all the members of my team (if they have been hired already) in order to get to know them better, understand their perspectives, and get a sense for the short-term tasks that await us.

5. Planning and Estimating

1) How do you define S-curve? What does S-curve entail?

Answer:

An *S-curve* is a cumulative display of cost, hours, or any other variable plotted against time. There are different types of S-curves which a project manager may encounter and utilize, including the following:

- Baseline
  - Reflects planned progress and may require revision if project requirements change
- Target
  - Reflects the ideal progress that will be made if all tasks are completed as expected
- Actual
  - Reflects actual progress to date
  - Can be compared with the Baseline and Target S curves in order to evaluate how the project is progressing

- Value & Percentage
  - All S curves may be graphed either as absolute values vs. Time or as a percentage vs. Time
  - Value vs. Time is useful for Cost or Man Hours S Curves
  - Percentage vs. Time is useful for Baseline, Target, and Actual S curves
- Cost vs. Time
  - Good for projects containing both labor and non-labor tasks
- Man Hours vs. Time
  - Good for labor-intensive projects

Also, be prepared to discuss growth, contraction, and slippage, as these are fundamental components of S curves.

2) Explain *cost performance index* (CPI). As a PM, how do you track CPI and how do you control it?

Answer: CPI is a measure of the efficiency of project expenditures. This is a ratio of earned value (i.e. the value of the work done so far) and actual cost (i.e. the actual amount spent on the project).

A CPI value above 1 (where the earned value is greater than the actual cost) is favorable, as this means the project is doing well against the budget. A CPI value of less than 1 means that the project is exceeding the budget.

When the budget has been exceeded, controlling measures must be taken. An earned value analysis (EVA) must be conducted to determine how much the budget has run over. Corrective action must then be taken to restore efficiency.

3) What is schedule variance (SV)? How is SV used to control the schedule? How do you find SV in MS project?

Answer: Schedule variance gives you an idea about your project progress with respect to the planned schedule. It tells you whether your project is progressing as per the schedule, ahead of schedule, or behind schedule. In other words, it's the difference between planned schedule and actual progress.

It is calculated by subtracting planned value from earned value (EV-PV)

If your project is behind schedule you can take corrective measures to bring the project back on track. Potential solutions include resource leveling, schedule crashing, etc. However, the corrective measures depend on the cause of the variance.

You can find SV easily in MS project simply by adding an SV column in your schedule or generating an EVM report.

4) What is a *project network diagram*? How do you identify critical path?

Answer: A project network diagram is a type of graph or flow chart which shows the sequence of activities, generally depicted by blocks which are linked together to illustrate the logical sequence.

Critical path is the longest path on the network. It is the sequence of activities which add up to the longest duration. It helps in determining the shortest possible time required to complete the project.

Critical path can be identified in several ways:

- It is the longest path through the network diagram;
- It is the shortest duration in which the project can be completed;
- Tasks on the critical path have zero float (or slack); and
- A slip of one day for any task on the critical path will result in a one day slip of the overall project finish date.

5) You are working as a program manager on a business-critical program, and one of your project managers reports a severe risk on his project. This is going to impact the overall program goal. How would you handle this situation? Give me some examples of risks that you have seen in your projects.

<u>Answer:</u> The following are several ways in which this issue can be handled:

- Understand the project criticality and its impact on the overall program goal, as well as the portfolio

- Understand how the delay in that project will impact other projects
- Revisit the program plan and the subsidiary plans
- Report the issue to portfolio manager and the management
- Re-plan the program deliverables
- Intimate the information to dependent projects
- Set a new baseline

Please note that this answer could vary from project to project. Because large projects themselves are sometimes considered programs and are therefore tracked at program level, it is important to bear in mind the differences between a project and a program, as discussed in Section 3, Question 1.

Some examples of risk that most projects encounter are as follows:

- Requirements elicitation taking much longer than anticipated
- Requirements documentation is not granular enough for development

- Development made many assumptions during requirements documentation, therefore a lot of change requests are being made by the client
- The client only had a big picture understanding during requirements elicitation and is coming back with changes now that (s)he has a better understanding
- Quality assurance is going to take much more time that initially budgeted
- Key resources have left/gone on emergency leave and there might be delays
- Hardware or software licenses were not available on time
- Data migration from an old system is mapping over improperly, leading to a lot of production support tickets
- Delays are being caused by system performance issues which were not factored into initial estimates (e.g. slow response times, lack of security, bad code design, unstable system, etc.)

- UAT is taking longer than expected because the stakeholders do not have adequate time or do not have adequate training on the system

6) One of your team members suddenly goes on an emergency leave. He was working on a task which is due in a week. How will you handle this situation?

Answer: This is an example of unavoidable risk. You should indicate that you would revisit the schedule and revise it as appropriate. Acknowledge that this is a significant issue, and there is a high risk of not meeting the deadline. Explain that you will nevertheless try various approaches like using a backup, negotiating a reduced deliverable, or borrowing equivalent resources from other groups in order to overcome this challenge.

7) What are different types of risk response?

Answer: There are 4 types of risk response, as follows:

Risk mitigation: Reduce the impact of risk

Risk avoidance: Totally avoiding risk by opting for an alternative approach

Risk transfer: Transferring the risk and responsibility to someone else

Risk acceptance: Some risks which can't be avoided, mitigated, or transferred are accepted (e.g. natural disaster).

8) How do you calculate the score of a risk? In which phase of the project do you identify risks?

Answer: Risk identification is done in the beginning of the project, but is also an ongoing activity. Risks are identified throughout the project cycle and response is planned accordingly. Risk score is calculated based on the probability of a risk occurring and on its impact.

9) One of your most skilled key team members has resigned. How would you go about trying to retain this member?

Answer: This question has more than one answer. I must consider several factors, including the criticality of the project (s)he is working on, the notice period I must plan for replacement, whether my organization has a retention policy, etc.

I would first talk with the team member in question to determine why (s)he is leaving. There could be one or more reasons, such as compensation, work-life balance, relocation, any number of personal reasons (e.g. sick spouse or child), etc. I would then do my best to find a resolution that would meet the team member's needs while allowing me to keep him/her on board. For example, if the issue was compensation, I could reach out to my seniors to determine whether an increase was merited and in the budget.

While there is no guarantee that efforts to retain the team member will be successful, the important thing is that I do my utmost to achieve retention.

Additionally, this situation illustrates the importance of succession planning. I always try to avoid situations where there is a very high dependency on only one or two key resources. In the even such a dependency does arise, I immediately begin succession planning for those individuals by initiating knowledge transfers or grooming others to become equivalents. There are many factors outside my control, and I might not always be successful in retaining top talent. Additionally, there might be budget cuts which affect my key resources. Therefore, it a golden rule to always have a plan B and backups for key team members.

10) Tell me about your experience in working with SOWs.

Answer: SOW is a widely-used term in the industry. It can stand for *scope of work* or *statement of work,* both of which can be used interchangeably.

A statement of work is a summary which explains the purpose of the project, as well as its desired results. The SOW contains many details including specifics of timing, exact scope of service or product deliverables, human resources that will be committed, and other service level agreements that govern day to day executables.

As a project manager, I work with SOWs all the time. A lot of my projects have involved a dual shore vendor or a time and material vendor. In these circumstances, we do not start work without an SOW. The SOWs I have worked on have been for both fixed bid contracts and recurring contracts. There are a few key items that I always ensure are included in the SOW, because ultimately the vendor can be held accountable only against this document. It should always include the very specific high-level deliverables, the timelines, the cost involved, and the service level agreements.

11) What is scope creep? How is it different from gold plating? Explain with an example.

Answer: Scope creep is a change in scope after the stakeholder has gained a better understanding of the requirements. For example, we might have made certain assumptions about various aspects of the requirements (e.g. functionality, reporting, interfacing with other systems, data models, user interface etc.). However, it is difficult to be very precise about the scope unless you get into more detail. You always start with a high-level scope and high-level estimate and allow for a 10-15% variance. Scope creep occurs when you move forward with the project, and upon further analysis find that more items are being added to the scope which can jeopardize the timelines.

Gold plating happens when people think of a great improvement to the product and rush to implement it without determining its impact. It is the act of doing additional work without considering its impact.

An example of gold plating could include the following: A programmer adds a feature the client did not request. The programmer's intention might be to impress the client, but the client is not willing to pay for work she did not request. This is perfectly fine in situations where you are confident that a) the client will love the change and b) it won't affect your bottom line (i.e. budget and timelines). However, it can be risky, especially if the added feature is not minor. The best course of action is to make a recommendation or a suggestion first. Discuss it with the users and then implement the enhanced functionality.

12) What are the different types of vendor contracts you have worked with? Which one is most suitable for a buyer?

Answer: I have worked with the following types of contracts:

Cost reimbursable (or cost plus): In these contracts, the vendor provides an itemized bill of their expenses, and also allocates for some profit. I would prefer this type of contract if there are many indirect costs on the vendor which might not always be very visible to us. It does shift some risk on the buyer for non-performance, but it is more of a shared risk between us and the vendor.

Time and material: I've used these contracts exclusively for temporary staffing positions. It is particularly useful if I have a position open where we would ideally want to hire the person after a certain period of time. Typically, I prefer a 1 year or an 18-month contract-to-hire position. However, on the flip side, it is expensive in the short term, as the billing is hourly, and also risky because there is no SLA or guarantee of performance. In this situation, our best hedge against hiring a wrong candidate is to ensure a very thorough interview process. If that fails, then we as a client will have to bear the cost.

Fixed price: This is the best contract for the buyer and puts a lot of risk on the selling vendor. However, some vendors do use it as a means of getting a foot in the door with a new buyer. This is one step beyond a free pilot.

Here the vendor defines a contract with all the details and provides a fixed bid to complete it. If the vendor is unable to complete the contract on time, then the entire cost of the extra hours is taken on by the vendor. I personally would always prefer a fixed bid on turnkey projects, but it's not always possible. Additionally, there is always a possibility of vendors lowballing just to get the contract, and if it's a critical time-bound project then there is a huge risk of not meeting the deadlines if the vendor is unable to complete on time. The buyer must, therefore, have a very good evaluation process and ask a lot of questions if there is a fear that the vendor has not understood the scope fully.

13) What is a T&M contract? To whom is it beneficial – the buyer or the seller? Why?

Answer: *T&M* refers to a time and material contract (as described briefly in the preceding question) where the buyer pays for all the time and material spent and used by the seller. An example of T&M is: Material cost plus $50/hr. for labor.

T&M is generally used for smaller projects. It is beneficial for the seller because the buyer does not have direct control of the money (s)he is spending. Also, the buyer must keep track daily of the deliverables (work done) in order to keep the project flowing smoothly. It also requires auditing of all seller invoices, thus increasing the buyer's efforts.

14) What are lead and lag? When do you add lead or lag to your schedule?

Answer: Lag time is when you purposely put a delay between the predecessor task and the successor. For example, a lead singer sings the first line, and the musicians wait until he finishes the first line before joining him.

Lead time, as the name suggests, is the time you allocate to preparing a subsequent task while you complete the task at hand. For example, you start heating your main course before you finish your appetizer.

15) What is WBS? Elaborate on how you would go about creating one.

Answer: WBS stands for *work breakdown structure*. It entails the deconstruction of the project into phases, deliverables, and work packages.

WBS is displayed in the form of a tree structure. It is hierarchical and incremental, and it provides a framework for your detailed project cost estimation. Please note that WBS is not a plan or a schedule. It simply lists what needs to be done; it does not specify the how and when.

Depending on how technical you are, there are various ways of breaking down the work required for a project:

- The first level is always a high-level milestone-driven plan. This includes the key deliverables and steps that need to be completed along the way. The PMO offers a framework of how to enter this in a system like Clarity or HP PPM.

- The second level is always a functional breakdown. You can look at your functional and non-functional requirements and allocate bodies of work to fulfill them. The grouping should be based on a combination of requirement priority, logical grouping of the requirements, and ease of implementation. This can be maintained in a tool like Microsoft Project or its equivalent.

- The next level is based on the technology design. This is much more hands-on and technical in nature. Here you need to break down the functional tasks into granular tasks that the development team can use to build the code. The rule of thumb is that if you have any task greater than 3 days, it needs to be broken down further.

16) What is RACI matrix? What is its use? Have you used it in your project?

Answer: This is a matrix for roles and responsibilities. RACI stands for "Responsible, Accountable, Consulted, and Informed." It's a simple table where tasks are listed down the side and the level of responsibility that each person or role has for each of the activities or responsibilities are laid out against it.

This matrix is also called a RAM (responsibility assignment matrix). Its main purpose is to quickly identify who is responsible for a given task and who else needs to be kept informed about the task/ activity. This is created and maintained by business analysts in my project and I oversee it.

17) What are the triple constraints? Explain with an example.

Answer: These are well-known constraints on the project: Time, Cost, and Scope. They are sometimes referred to as the project management triangle.

An example of triple constraints might occur when you are about to deliver a key deliverable, and the client comes up with a very critical change request. All three constraints would be present in this situation. It would be very important to be tactical here by negotiating with the client for early delivery in the next week or providing a temporary workaround and then taking up the change request for the next planned delivery.

18) What do you mean by stakeholders? When do you identify stakeholders in your project? Where do you define their involvement or the frequency of communication with them?

<u>**Answer:**</u> In very simple words, stakeholders could be anyone who has an interest in the outcome of the project. The outcome could be positive or negative. Stakeholder identification occurs during the project initiation.

The PM defines the frequency of communication within the communication management plan. RACI matrix is also useful to define which things must be communicated to whom.

Stakeholders in my projects have been the subject matter experts from the business side, business side and technology side management, representatives from the systems that are impacted by my project, and, finally, my own technology team.

19) Which subsidiary plans do you consider while preparing a PM plan?

Answer: I always consider the following subsidiary plans:

- Integration management plan
- Scope management plan
- Risk management plan
- Time management plan
- Procurement management plan
- Cost management plan
- HR management plan
- Quality management plan
- Communication management plan

20) How do you differentiate between product scope and project scope? Give an example.

Answer: A product is the outcome of a project. It is the final software application that will be used by the business. Product scope is essentially the functional and non-functional requirements and implementation specifications of the application.

A project is the set of actions or activities that is needed to deliver the product. In order to successfully deliver the product, project scope must include budgeting, planning, staffing, resource management, project monitoring, and reporting.

To put it simply: Product scope tells us what the customer wants, and project scope tells us how we are going to do it.

Example: Imagine you are assigned as PM on a data center project. Product scope would be computers, servers, office space, network connectivity, requisite software, etc. The overall product would be the data center.

Project scope, in this case, would be everything that you do to convert an empty space into a fully functional data center. It would cover all the requirements gathering, vendor contracts, scope documentation, planning, execution etc.

21) What is LOE? How does it differ from estimate and ROM?

Answer: LOE stands for *level of effort.* It is typically defined in person hours or person days. It is one of the primary tasks of the PM.

LOE is simply an estimate. When you estimate work, you are outlining approximately what you are going to spend (time or cost).

ROM stands for *rough order of magnitude.* It's a very high-level estimate which can be around plus or minus 20% of the LOE or estimate.

When you get a high-level scope, you use ROM. When you have a detailed scope, you use LOE.

22) It is often said that a PM spends 90% of her time on communication. Do you agree? What are your different communication channels?

Answer: Yes. A PM spends the vast majority of his or her time on communication; 90% might be high, so I would say more like 65%. Some communication channels I utilize are as follows:

- Team meetings
- Status reports

- Stakeholder interactions
- Follow-ups
- Handling escalations
- Interdepartmental communications
- Interviews
- Management meetings

23) What is a *project management information system (PMIS)*?

Answer:

An organization's PMIS is a part of enterprise environmental factors. It includes all the automated tools (any software or other tool that might be in use; e.g. scheduling tool), CM system, work authorization software, time tracking software, procurement management software, etc.

24) What are the different types of costs?

Answer:

Variable cost: This cost changes with the amount of production or the amount of work (e.g. cost of material, supplies, etc.).

Fixed cost: These are costs which do not change with production changes (e.g. setup cost, rent, utilities, etc.).

Direct Cost: These costs are directly attributable to the work on the project (e.g. team travels, recognition, etc.).

Indirect Cost: These are overhead items (e.g. taxes, fringe benefits, etc.).

25) Please explain the 50/50 and 20/80 rules.

Answer: *This question is likely to appear when the role and responsibilities include scheduling and planning. It's one of the most important questions you will come across. – KG*

These rules are used in progress reporting, at the work package level, where work packages are completed relatively quickly and frequently.

50/50: Here activity is considered 50% complete when it begins, and credit for the remaining 50% is given only when it is completed.

20/80: Similar to the above, here activity is 20% completed when it begins, and credit for remaining 80% is given when it is completed.

Note: There is also a 0/100 rule where activity gets credit only when it is completed.

26) What is *marginal analysis*?

Answer: Marginal analysis compares the cost of incremental improvements to the increased revenue obtained from quality improvements. In other words, when quality does not provide added value, you should stop trying to improve quality. Marginal analysis is done to identify this point.

27) What is *level-0 DFD*?

Answer: Level-0 DFD is the highest abstraction level, and is also known as context level DFD. It depicts the entire information system as one diagram concealing all the underlying details.

28) What is *COCOMO model*?

Answer: COCOMO is a well-known model for software cost estimation. Program or code size is expressed in terms of number of lines of code (SLOC, KLOC). It stands for *constructive cost estimation model*. This model is structured in two parts: COCOMO-1 and COCOMO -2.

If you are an expert in estimation using this model, you can elaborate more. However, this model is no longer widely used, so detailed information is not necessary unless you have working experience in the same. – KG

29) What would you do if you found out that a contractor was in a conflict of interest situation?

Answer: I would escalate this to my superior immediately. Although the success of my project is important, ethical integrity is of the utmost importance. My role is such that I am an extension of the company, and it is my duty to make every effort to protect the company from liability.

30) Give me an example of a win-win situation you have negotiated.

Answer: *You should try to come up with your own example, but a generic example is provided here as well. – KG*

Example: I took on a project where the client wanted to implement a repair. This repair would allow us to pass inspection, but my client felt it would be an inadequate solution for the long term. I suggested utilizing an old product for one area and then using a new product that would cost the same amount of money as the initial repair cost. The client got more than he asked for, and my job was completed quicker, saving both time and money.

6. Project Execution

1) What do you think is the difference between Risks and Issues? During which phase of your project do you identify issues and risks? How do you control it?

Answer: *This is a very common question in interviews.*

An **issue** is something which *is* occurring or *will* occur, while a **risk** is something which *may* occur.

Example: Let's assume that the data migration from an older system to a new system is a very complex effort with five (5) dependencies which must happen in a very specific way. Say one of these five things does not go as planned. In this instance, there is a risk to the timely completion of the data migration effort. However, if the situation plays out such that the deadline is actually missed, then the risk becomes an issue.

There is no particular phase in which risks and issues are identified. These are ongoing activities.

You should identify and respond to risks and issues throughout the project lifecycle.

You control risks and issues by designing the mitigation plan to reduce their impact (the plan will depend on the type of risks). Some risks which are beyond your control are to be accepted.

2) You are in the execution phase of a project, and suddenly the customer comes up with a change request. You identify that this change will impact the cost as well as schedule. How will you respond to the customer to make the situation win-win?

<u>Answer:</u> I would typically do the following:

- Conduct an overall impact analysis of the change request to determine the specific impact on schedule and cost
- Analyze the dependencies while implementing (executing) change request (CR)
- Figure out an alternate way to deploy the requested change in two or more phases without affecting the earlier schedule

3) What do you mean by residual risk?

Answer: Residual risk is a kind of risk which is left over after natural or inherent risk have been reduced by risk controls. In other words, it's the amount of danger left, after taking all the control measures.

Example: We know there are too many permutations and combinations to test in a process flow engine that we are trying to build. We also know that the QA team is a centralized shared resource and is not a subject matter expert. Additionally, the time allocated for QA efforts is too short.

Here, we know that there is a risk of not being able to complete quality assurance on time and cover all the required permutations. Thus, to mitigate this risk, we take certain measures such as facilitating in-depth knowledge transfers to the QA team and creating very efficient test scripts that test the maximum functionality in minimal time.

Despite these efforts, some risk will remain because of the time and complexity factors. That is the residual risk.

4) What is schedule crashing? When do you apply crashing to your schedule? How does it affect your project?

Answer: Schedule crashing is a last-ditch effort to meet your deadline by allocating more resources to the project. When you crash a schedule to meet your deadline, you don't have to crash all the activities. The important thing to note here is that the activities which impact the schedule are those which have zero float (i.e. activities on the critical path).

Crashing a schedule would result in extra cost due to additional resources being allocated. Also, schedule crashing does not always lead to activities being completed earlier. The activities which have nothing to do with resource allocation cannot be crashed.

5) What are the different types of conflict resolution? Which type do you feel is most widely used?

Answer: The following are the different types of conflict resolution:

Confronting: Includes identifying the underlying concerns of the opponents and finding an alternative which meets each party's concerns. This is also known as 'win-win' or 'collaborating.'

Withdrawing: This is when a person does not pursue her/his own concerns or those of the opponent. This is also known as 'avoiding.'

Forcing: An individual firmly pursues his or her own concerns despite the resistance of the other person.

Compromising: Utilizes a mutually acceptable solution which partially satisfies both parties.

I find that confronting is the most widely used technique, as it is the most favorable to both parties.

6) Where do you deposit your project documents? Do you have KT ("Knowledge Transfer") documents which a new member of the team can use as reference? How do you ensure a smooth transition?

<u>**Answer:**</u> *Here, the answer should ideally be SharePoint site or (if you have one) your own repository. If it is a SharePoint site, you keep all your project-related documents in different folders. You will likely be questioned as to how you find the version history of the document. -KG*

For my projects, I typically have well-organized SharePoint sites aligned with each phase of the project. I use links to these SharePoint sites in my communications so that all the team members and management have access. There are different folders named appropriately for different purposes, so it is never difficult to find any information you need. It might sound like something minor and commonsensical, but it's the sum of all parts that makes a project easy to execute and keeps it organized.

I highly recommend maintaining all knowledge documents like business case, project plan, high-level and detailed business requirements, and functional specifications for any project in these share point sites. Additionally, any domain-related documentation or process documentation or training PPTs are also maintained. For Agile projects, there might not be such extensive documentation, but we still have user stories, wireframes, and other related documents.

7) What is halo effect? Have you seen any examples of it within your organization or in your project?

Answer: Halo effect is something that happens when you put someone in a position they can't handle, just because they're good at another job.

Example: A programmer from your team is promoted to project manager just because he knows the technology better. However, he struggles with the PM job because he lacks project management skills.

8) **Explain "Theory X" and "Theory Y" managers. Imagine you are a team member working under a Theory X manager. How would you adjust yourself to deal with him?**

Answer: Theory X and Theory Y are theories of human motivation and management. A Theory X manager is someone who does not like to give complete independence to the team. She prefers to monitor things closely. In other words, a Theory X manager does not trust the team.

Theory Y is the reverse of this. A Theory Y manager trusts his team. It is much easier to be a Theory Y manager. According to Theory Y, your team won't let you down if you trust them.

If you're working with a Theory X manager, it is best to show both patience and pro-activeness. Explain to your manager that if you need his help you will definitely reach out to him. Bring to his attention the fact that frequent distractions from your work affect overall productivity.

9) How do you define quality? When you prepare for quality management, what are the goals that you keep in mind?

Answer: Quality is the degree to which a set of inherent characteristics fulfills requirements. Note that quality comes at a cost. In other words, you must spend money to get better quality (this is called "cost of quality", or "COQ").

During quality management planning you must understand/address the following points:

- Quality management includes creating and following policies and procedures that meet
  the project's defined quality needs.
- The goal of quality management is to ensure that the specified approach to quality is implemented on the project.
- There are 3 aspects of quality management:
    o Quality planning
    o Quality assurance

o Quality control

10) What is cost of quality? What measures do you take to control COQ?

Answer: In simple words, cost of quality is the amount of money you spend to make your project right.

To calculate your project's COQ, you must calculate all the costs associated with quality-related activities.

There are a few ways to control COQ. It is always cheaper to find bugs/defects earlier in the project than later, and there are always quality costs associated with everything your project produces (production defects). Cost of quality is just a way of tracking the cost of those activities.

11) What is the difference between quality assurance (QA) and quality control (QC)?

Answer: As the name states, quality assurance is the act of instilling confidence in a product or service, whereas quality control is an evaluation to indicate needed corrective responses. Simply put, quality assurance is a failure prevention system and quality control is a failure detection system.

QA defines the standards or methodology which must be followed to meet customer requirements, whereas QC ensures that the defined standards are followed at every step.

12) As a PM, do you strive for quality or quantity? How do you explain this to your team? Do you find that there are conflicting views on this within your team?

Answer: Any PM would expect both quality and quantity. In other words, faster and better service to the customer. Productivity should be maximized and defect density or defect leakage should be minimized.

I generally explain this to my team by emphasizing the importance of the customer to any service provider. Revenue comes from customers, so satisfied customers are the top priority for any service provider.

There typically are not conflicting views on this within the team unless the productivity or defect density goals are unrealistic. However, the goals you set for your project should be based on historical data and geared toward slight improvement. In other words, goals should be well-founded and achievable.

13) How do you carry out failure factor analysis while managing risks?

Answer: *This question is another way of asking how you carry out Root Cause Analysis (RCA). The purpose of this question is to determine whether you know how to find the causes of failures. It's not only about project failure, but failure in meeting your project goals or a slippage in any tasks, deliverables, etc. - KG*

There are different methods of conducting RCA. Typically, the analysis is carried out as follows:

- Identify & define the problem
- Collect data (i.e. proof, duration, and impact of the problem)

- Analyze causal factors (i.e. sequence of events leading to the problem, conditions that allow the problem, co-occurring problems, etc.)
- Identify the root cause(s)
  o Using the same tools you used in the previous step, identify the roots of each causal factor
- Recommend and implement solution(s) (i.e. ways to prevent problem from reoccurring, procedure for implementing solution(s), risks of implementing solution(s), etc.)

14) Your customer decides in the middle of execution that they want the project to be completed 10 days earlier than planned. How will you handle this situation?

Answer: I would not be able to commit right away to any change in schedule. I've worked on many projects where timelines have been driven, not by the length of the tasks, but by management goals or regulatory needs. Even in these instances, we need to plan intelligently and propose a realistic date based on the current resource situation.

If a client requests an earlier deliverable in the middle of a project, I would first ask them to provide a strong business reason. I would then work with management to understand whether the business reason is valid; if it is, then we would need to evaluate our current task list, resources, and readiness.

Before committing to an earlier date, I would evaluate whether:

- Activities can be overlapped or organized more efficiently to accelerate the process;
- Any feature or functionality can be sacrificed to achieve the accelerated timeframe;
- A small portion of each task can be cut down in order to leave some things to chance but still deliver the project;
- Additional resources may be able to help, and how quickly those resources can be obtained; and
- There is a scope for the current team working overtime and weekends for a limited time.

15) You have been working on a cost plus incentive fees (CPIF) contract project.

The estimated cost is \$200K, and there is a predetermined fee of \$20K with a buyer-to-seller ratio of 70/30. The actual cost of the project was \$120K. Would you be able to calculate the total amount received by the seller?

<u>Answer:</u> Yes. You should be able to calculate this from the given data.

You first need to break the data down as follows:

- Estimated cost: \$200K
- Actual cost: \$120K
- Predetermined fees: \$20K
- Seller portion of buyer-to-seller ratio: 30%
- Net savings (i.e. estimated cost – actual cost): \$80K

The total amount earned by the seller is the actual cost of the project + the seller portion of the net savings + predetermined fees. Here, this is calculated as follows:

$$\$120K + \$24K + \$20K = \$164K$$

This has less to do with the calculations and more to do with your understanding of the CPIF contract type and how it works.

16) What are a contract and a supplier in ITIL?

Answer:

Contract: A legally binding agreement between two parties.

Supplier: The third party responsible for supplying goods or services.

In most of my projects, we have had a combination of internal teams and teams from the I.T. vendors. I have worked with most tier 1 and some tier 2 vendors and am well versed with how contract life cycle and vendor management works.

17) What are proactive and reactive changes?

Answer:

Proactive change: Change made for business benefits. Improves service and cost efficiency. (E.g. introduction of new servers to scale up the network.)

Reactive change: Change requested by the business stakeholder based on their everyday usage (e.g. change a particular query structure of a report or the fields on a particular screen).

18) What is a work authorization system?

Answer: Work authorization system is used to approve all project work throughout the course of the current project management venture.

Be prepared to discuss whether you've used this on past projects and how you feel about it. - KG

19) You are assigned as project manager to a new project for a customer who is known to request numerous changes. What would you do at the beginning of the project to manage this customer?

Answer: I have worked on a lot of projects where the customer requests significant changes late in the game. It would be unfair to always blame them for lack of foresight or planning, as sometimes it is not in their control. Changes in regulations, company policy, and economic situation, for example, are not always foreseeable and may necessitate changes to the project once it is underway. It is always important to see things from a customer's perspective, as it is ultimately the client who is footing the bill for your team.

That being said, it is also important to protect oneself from Service Level Agreements (SLA) violations or being labeled a slacker.

When working with vendors I typically spend a lot of time defining a contract and ensuring that all parties have signed it. If I am a vendor project manager, it is even more important for me because my company might have to absorb the cost if I do a poor job of defining SLAs. Once the SLAs are defined, the scope and requirements must be crystal clear. This is easier with waterfall style development, but sometimes tricky for Agile. However, even in Agile, we leave a scope of what we call "iteration zero" where these nuances can be managed before the development begins.

Next, it is very important to define a change management protocol and reduce it to signed documentation. This document will contain the definition of what constitutes a change vs. a defect. Our commitment should be that we will absorb the defects found in the budget and timeline allocated, but we are not responsible for any change requests. We should clarify that while we are more than happy to accommodate change requests if the clients absolutely need them, this will consume more time and money.

Finally, I always try to model things as visually as possible - preferably with working prototypes if we have the skill and time. This is because most changes are requested because the customers themselves were not very clear on what they wanted in the product. This is simply a human limitation: unless you can see the product and play around with it, you are not able to visualize it completely. To mitigate these types of changes we should be as visual as possible during requirements gathering stage, utilizing proper wireframes at a minimum, and working prototypes if time permits.

I've found that the above techniques are good safeguards against change requests when they do appear.

20) You have been assigned as PM for a project that is halfway through execution. You meet the customer and inform him that the project is within the baselines, but the customer informs you that he is not happy with the performance. What would you do to investigate this matter?

<u>Answer</u>: A project manager's worst nightmare is hearing these words. However, we all hear them at one point or another, and the ability to deal with unhappy clients is a cornerstone of the PM skillset. It's important not to jump into assigning blame to yourself or your team. Instead, the key is to understand *why* the client is unhappy and determine what you can do to fix the situation.

Here are some reasons a customer may be unhappy with a product, and ways I would go about resolving the matter:

- The functionality has not been delivered as per specifications.
  - Anything that does not meet pre-defined specifications is a defect, and there could be many factors that led to such defect (e.g. insufficient QA, misunderstanding on the part of the technology team, etc.).
  - In this scenario, I would accept the team's shortcomings and promise the customer that the issue will be resolved ASAP.
- The product is not intuitive enough or does not navigate smoothly.
  - In this case, I would shadow the client's usage of the tool to understand what exactly is not intuitive and what can be changed to make it better.
  - I would determine and explain to the client what can and cannot be accommodated in the release. The items that cannot be accommodated should be captured in a document so they can be addressed in subsequent releases.

- Bad nonfunctional performance of the system.
  - Often, we focus too much on functionality, and nonfunctional requirements get ignored in the process. These are requirements like reliability, scalability, performance, security, data retention, etc. that are not directly visible to a daily user but are very important for optimal running of the system and overall user experience. A lot of times these get overlooked and focus is on functionality only. If any of the non-functional parameters are not working as desired I will get to the exact reasons why the system function is sub-optimal and remedy the situation by working with whichever group is responsible for that particular non-functional feature.

21) How do you ensure traceability in your project?

Answer: I always maintain a well-organized requirements traceability matrix (RTM) in my projects. RTM is a process of documenting the links between the requirements and the work products developed to implement and verify those requirements.

The RTM captures all requirements and their traceability in a single document delivered at the conclusion of the life cycle.

You use RTM to reference each work product from the requirements phase until the delivered product.

RTM includes:

- Requirement ID
- Risks
- Requirement Type
- Requirement Description
- Trace to Design Specification
- Unit Test Cases
- Integration Test Cases
- System Test Cases
- User Acceptance Test Cases
- Trace to Test Script

22) What is risk register? What are the different fields in your risk register?

Answer: Risk register is the tool used for documenting all the risks identified in your project and additional information about each identified risk. The different fields include risk description, status, category, owner, mitigation/response plan, reference, probability, etc.

Risk register is a live document which is updated whenever a new risk is identified.

23) What are the different leadership styles? What style you think you follow?

Answer: *This question comes up for senior managers or people who are experienced PMPs (project management professionals). - KG*

The different styles of leadership are as follows:

Authoritarian/Autocratic: Gives clear direction and expects compliance.

Participative/Democratic: Offers guidance to team members, but also encourages participation.

Delegation (laissez-faire): Offers little or no guidance to the team and believes in "letting them be."

As a project manager, you need to establish a leadership style that matches the needs of the team. I typically base my style on the experience and skill level of the team for the respective function.

If it is a very junior team that relies on me for getting a clear picture on the nuances of their task, then I would follow a slightly authoritarian style. I would, however, always advise against an autocratic style that goes into the territory of micromanagement.

If it is a mid-level team, then I would use a democratic approach, as it's best to delegate effectively and provide some governance framework. I would keep track of deliverables and deadlines, but might not be involved in granular tasks.

If it is a very senior team, then the delegation style works best because the expectation is that the people already know their tasks very well. The project manager only needs to get involved for escalations and risks, but otherwise should not get in people's way.

24) How do you calculate the number of channels in your project? If there are 5 members on your project team, how many communication channels would there be?

Answer: The number of communication channels is calculated by $N*(N-1)/2$, where "N" represents number of resources including PM.

In this case, there are 6 resources (5 team members and you as PM). Note that people often forget to count the PM in the number of resources/ it is very important to include the PM in this calculation.

Here the answer would be: $6*5/2=15$

25) What are the different types of service providers that you have worked with on your projects?

Answer: I've worked with a few different types of service providers, including the following:

Internal service provider: These are internal development teams that are formed for specific projects. For example, if there is a project sanctioned for 2 years for a regulatory product to be built and customized in Java/J2EE technologies, then the project manager can decide to form the team using the company's internal resources instead of working with a vendor to deliver it.

Shared services provider: These are teams that are a part of the same organization and are maintained as shared services across the department. The ones most commonly used are business analysis and process center of excellence, a centralized QA team, a data team, or teams that have expertise around specific software applications or platforms. For example, a firm might have a SharePoint center of excellence, a BPM center of excellence, etc.

External service provider: Sometimes it makes more sense to outsource the project to an external vendor. These are complex decisions that involve a combination of criteria like cost, expertise, expected duration, company policy, time to market, and resource availability. Once a decision is made to go ahead with a vendor, there are many steps to be taken, such as request for information, request for proposal, working with vendor management, getting a vendor onboard, and coordinating with the vendor for project deliverables. Working with a vendor is a very different equation that having an own team. There must be very effective delegation and tracking of deliverables. Sometimes hard negotiations might also be involved, as we are paying a third party.

26) How do you define a PM's role in project risk management?

Answer: The project manager has special responsibilities in the risk management process. As a PM, you have overall responsibility for delivering a successful project which fully meets project objectives. In risk management, a PM's role may include:

- Encouraging senior management to support risk management activities
- Consulting with stakeholders to determine the acceptable level of risk
- Developing a risk management plan
- Promoting a risk management process for the assigned project
- Approving risk responses and associated actions before implementation

27) Give one example where one of your team members was not willing to take up a task due to lack of motivation, and explain what you did as a PM to resolve the issue.

Answer: *This is a situation-based question designed to evaluate your managerial skills. You want to showcase how you determine the appropriate motivation strategies for your staff members by understanding their different needs and perspectives. Be sure to touch on the communication of goals and visions to your staff, gaining commitment to these goals, establishing appropriate reward and incentive structures, and supporting and leading staff to success. - KG*

Examples:

- The employee might be underperforming because of a personal problem.
  - In this case, it is best to not get into details of the problem unless the information is voluntarily given. The employee might just need some space at that time. However, we should keep a

close eye on how much time the employee needs to get back on track, and we must determine whether the situation poses any risk to the project.

- The employee might have hit a wall in terms of learning or might be bored in the current role.
  - In this situation, a PM should try to work with the employee to create opportunities for learning or assuming new responsibilities. The goal is to motivate the employee and reignite their passion and drive.
- The employee might be dissatisfied with compensation, work environment, governance, or administrative issues.
  - In this situation, it is best to not overpromise, but just acknowledge that there is a problem. This is because a lot of things that the employee might think is in your control might not be. For example, things like compensation, work visas, and promotions likely flow largely, if not primarily, through HR; only a

small portion of those decisions typically lie directly in the hands of the manager. Hence, you should not promise anything directly, but instead, assure the person that you will look into it and support them with whatever is in your power to make it happen.

- The employee might be demotivated because of hierarchy or office politics.
  - o Once again here, understanding the root cause is very important. This could include two people not working well together, someone not being happy with the management, etc. It's important to keep the lines of communication open to understand the issue as fully as possible. Can it be remediated? Can it be avoided? Based on this analysis, a logical middle ground must be found, as there are no silver bullets for situations like this.

28) What is value chain analysis?

Answer: Value-chain analysis is a strategic analysis tool used to better understand the firm's competitive advantage, to identify where the value to customers can be increased or costs reduced, and to better understand the firm's linkages with suppliers, customers, and other firms in the industry. The activities include all steps necessary to provide a competitive product or service to the customer.

The term value chain is used because each activity is intended to add value to the product or service for the customer. Management can better understand the firm's competitive advantage and strategy by separating its operations according to activity.

29) What is sunk cost? Would you close a project halfway through because sunk cost was very high?

Answer: Sunk cost is expended cost which will never have any value.

Example: You are working on a project which has an initial budget of $ 1M. You are halfway through the project and you have already spent $ 2M and the end does not seem near. Would you consider the fact that you are already over budget by $ 1M when determining whether to continue with the project? No. Whatever money you spent is gone. Sunk cost should not be considered when deciding whether to continue the troubled project. Instead, the question should be whether the benefit of completing the project will outweigh the additional cost that it is going to consume.

30) How do you manage a diverse team towards the common project goal?

Answer: I would stick to the basics of project management. Focus on your ability to delegate in a fair and practical way, clearly define project roles and responsibilities, keep personality clashes and conflict to a minimum, and provide feedback to the project team.

For this question, outline your management style and explain why it works. Be prepared to give an example if requested. – KG

31) How does scheduling help in executing a project?

Answer: *This question is looking for an answer based on actual scheduling and project monitoring experience. Be prepared to provide an example. - KG*

When the activity effort and resource estimates are known, getting the work done depends on the sequence of the tasks.

Dependencies on the tasks need to be clearly known. Unconnected tasks/activities can often be sequenced in a parallel manner to reduce project time. This is all possible through scheduling. Scheduling is done from the activities list prepared after work breakdown structure (WBS) has been finalized. Scheduling is also important for reminding people of deadlines and having clear communication as to who owns which task.

32) Tell me about one of the largest or most important projects you managed for your previous organization.

Answer: *The answer could vary as per your previous experience. You can describe any project that you have managed previously. Please make sure you are covering few of the following items in your answer:*

- Project vision
- Project scope
- Your management approach

- Project outcome
- Lessons learned – both positive and negative

33) Please describe autocratic and bureaucratic leadership.

Answer:

Autocratic Leadership: Also known as authoritarian leadership. This is a leadership style characterized by individual control over all decisions and little input from group members. These types of leaders make choices based on their own ideas and judgments, and they rarely accept advice from followers.

Bureaucratic Leadership: This style of leadership follows a close set of standards. Everything is done in an exact, specific way to ensure safety and/or accuracy. Bureaucratic leadership is generally used in situations where the work environment is dangerous and specific sets of procedures are necessary to ensure safety.

34) How do you know if your resources are over-allocated? How would you manage over allocation?

Answer: If you are developing a schedule properly, performing effort estimations at the task level, and assigning resources, you will be able to detect over-allocation from within the schedule. In the real world, you would notice things such as a resource constantly working extra hours, appearing tired and stressed, allowing their deliverables to start slipping past their targeted due dates, etc.

Short term over-allocations are manageable. Long term over-allocations can cause severe problems with the team morale, the quality of work and the environment, and could even result in individuals leaving the organization. In these instances, you can take measures such as assigning some of the work to another individual, delaying the start and targeted completion of some of the work, and maybe even removing the scope of work altogether.

7. Project Monitoring and Controlling

1) How do you control changes in your project? Do you use a change control mechanism?

Answer: *You should discuss CCB (change control board) in response to this question. CCB is a body which evaluates change requests and decides whether to approve them based on the current project status and other dependent factors. – KG*

In my projects, I always have a change control board post-signoff. This board has people from the business side and technology side. Any requirement change requested post-signoff or during production is always validated by this board. Factors that are considered are impact, cost, number of people affected, urgency, and technical feasibility. Only changes that are approved by the board are taken up for estimation and development.

2) Do you have vendor management experience? Does your team have

vendor resources? What is a major challenge that you've observed in managing your resources and vendor resources?

Answer: Ideally you will answer "yes" to the first two parts of this question, as vendor management is a necessary skill for a project manager. Even if you are employed by a vendor company, it still important to know how vendor management works because you will be using that skill to manage client expectations.

The essential steps for vendor management are listed below. You can use this list a guideline, filling in with examples from your project.

- **RFI process**
  - This is the first step where you request information from the various vendors you want to involve. Typically, big companies have a separate vendor management office, and the choice is restricted to vendors that are already on their list.
- **Request for proposal (RFP)**

o The shortlisted vendors provide an in-depth proposal explaining how they will deliver the project. This is a long, detail-oriented process. Various factors such as cost, offshore presence, expertise, development methodology, past successes, management preference, and relationships play into the final selection. There is usually scoring based on weighted criteria and lots of negotiations before a final choice is made.

- **Delivery begins**
  o A lot of ground work is required to establish specific plans for communication, task assignments, responsibilities, detailed SLAs, etc.

- **Continuous monitoring**
  o Throughout the project lifecycle, one must monitor the project closely and hold the vendor accountable for the deliverable. It is unwise to let go of all control, as you will ultimately be held responsible if the project fails.

Some major challenges I've observed are:

- Slow communication due to vendor resources not being located on your organization's premises
- Less authority on the vendor resources
  - This is optional/depends on the type of organization you are working with
- Frequent follow-ups with vendor resources and their account managers, less dedication to assignments, and diminished responsiveness
- Ambiguous clauses in SLAs
- Incorrect estimation because of eagerness to win the project
  - Such aggressive estimates always result in problems because timelines are communicated to management based on the vendor commitment

3) One or more of your team members comes to you to request specific training in order to deliver the project. You agree that the training is

necessary/beneficial. What will be your next steps?

Answer: *This type of question would be expected particularly if you are interviewing with a projectized organization. - KG*

If I agree that the training is necessary, I will check with the internal learning and development team to see if we have any trainings planned for the skills required and I will nominate the team members based on their availability and without affecting project delivery. If there are no trainings already planned, then I will need to seek management's approval for external trainings, explaining to them why the trainings are critical. If the trainings are project-specific, they will add to the cost of the project, so I must bear this in mind when planning to fulfill training requests.

4) **How do you calculate CPI (Cost Performance Index) and SPI (Schedule Performance Index)? How do you use these values to determine whether your project is under control?**

Answer:

CPI is calculated by as Earned Value divided by Actual Cost (EV/AC), while SPI is calculated as Earned Value divided by Perceived Value (EV/PV).

If CPI is greater than 1, it means EV is more than AC, which means that the project is doing well with respect to cost.

If SPI is greater than 1, it means PV is greater than EV, which means that the project is within the schedule.

5) **When your project status is yellow, approaching red, what steps or measures do you take to bring it back to green?**

Answer: My top priority would be to work on the plan I had initially. I'd commence root cause analysis to determine why the status was going to red. If it was a situation where I had not yet implemented the plan, I would start implementing immediately; if I had already implemented the plan and found it wasn't working out, I would do alternative analysis to come up with another plan to move the project back to green.

My approach would, of course, depend on the root cause(s) identified in RCA, which could range from vendor dependency to resource shortage, funding issues, etc.

6) What are the different performance metrics you use in your project? How do you track them?

Answer: *Performance metrics would be related to productivity and quality. Widely used productivity metrics are SPI and CPI, which were discussed in greater depth in question 4 above. For quality, we track defect density. Defect density is tracked by defects per function points (if you are using function point as an estimation technique). - KG*

7) How would you deal with a situation where there were many user defects logged during UAT, and your release to production was going to be delayed?

Answer: This depends on the type of project. For a fixed-schedule project, where the product should be released to production, I would need to deal with all the challenges to ensure release to production happened as per the timeline.

In other types of projects, it is possible to delay the release if there is no way to stabilize the situation.

In a worst-case scenario, I would plan (with approval from the stakeholders) to release the product on schedule with fixes being included in the next release. If possible, I would plan to deploy the patch or minor release just a week or two later in order to fix important user acceptance test bugs.

8) You are working as a PM on a small-scale project which has a duration of 3 months. The scope is fixed, and your team has started working on the design part. Suddenly the customer changes the requirements, which impacts both schedule and cost. What steps will you take?

<u>Answer:</u> Since the change is occurring during the initial phase of the project, I will route it through CCB, highlighting its impact on schedule and cost. If the change is approved, I will revise my plans and schedule.

Note that this question is gauging your knowledge of change control process, though it does not state this specifically. - KGo

9) What is earned value management (EVM)?

Answer: EVM is a methodology for objectively measuring project performance and progress and forecasting project outcome. Once you establish cost and schedule baseline, it becomes a great source for understanding project performance during execution. EVM helps answer questions like the following:

- Are we delivering more or less work than planned?
- When is the project likely to be completed?
- Are we currently over or under budget?
- What will be the cost of the remaining work?

10) What is net present value (NPV)?

Answer: NPV is the measurement of profitability of a project or undertaking.

It is the difference between the present value of cash inflow and present value of cash outflow over a period of time. NPV is determined by calculating the costs (negative cash flows) and benefits (positive cash flows) for each period of investment.

NPV is a key decision maker in project selection method. If NPV is less than one, it means the project is not going to add any value to the organization and may be rejected.

11) What are internal rate of return (IRR) and payback period?

Answer: IRR is a metric used in capital budgeting; it measures the profitability of potential investments.

Internal rate of return is a discount rate that makes the NPV of all cash flows from a project equal to zero.

The payback period is the length of time required to recover the cost of an investment.

The payback period of a given investment or project is an important determinant of whether to undertake the position or project, as longer payback periods are typically not desirable for investment positions.

12) Explain benefit-cost ratio (BCR).

Answer: BCR is a ratio which identifies the benefits of a project (expressed in monetary terms) relative to the costs of that project (also expressed in monetary terms). BCR is used in cost-benefit analysis to summarize the overall monetary value of a project or proposal.

13) While assessing your team members' performance, you find that some of them are not strong enough to handle their assigned tasks. How would you handle this situation?

Answer: This is a situation PMs face often; it is important to be proactive enough to talk with your team members.

I would first communicate that the improvement was needed and get feedback from the team member to better understand his/her challenges. I would then determine what kind of help was needed (e.g. mentoring, motivating, training, coaching, etc.) and establish a performance review and monitoring schedule.

14) What is a GANTT chart? How do you use it your project?

Answer: Gantt charts are very important tools used in project scheduling and tracking, reporting, etc.

Gantt charts illustrate the start and finish dates of the terminal elements and summary elements of a project. They show dependency on tasks and provide a graphical view of assigned resources, allocation, etc. Gantt charts also show the planned baseline (timeline) and the project progress (actual timeline).

15) What are the different techniques that you use when you are doing quantitative risk analysis?

Answer: When conducting quantitative risk analysis, I use the following tools: interviewing (asking questions to get required inputs), sensitivity analysis, simulation, and decision tree.

16) What is a bill of materials (BOM)? Do you have experiences working with bills of materials?

Answer: A bill of materials is a document which lists everything needed to deliver the product. It is a list of the raw materials, sub-assemblies, intermediate assemblies, sub-components, parts and the quantities of each needed to manufacture an end product.

A bill of materials is a centralized source of information used to manufacture a product. It is an engineering term that refers to the design of a product. Manufacturers that build products start the assembling process by creating a BOM.

The most common item that project managers think about when calculating the cost of a project is the cost of human resources. This can be determined by the hourly billing rate that is sourced from the rate chart maintained for different skills sets in most big companies. However, there are many other costs which must be considered. There are costs incurred because of shared resources; indirect costs like management expenses, software licenses, or real estate; recurring hardware and dedicated software license costs; and unexpected expenses like specialized consulting required only in times of emergency. These costs are all included in the bill of materials.

We typically create a cost plan at the end of the year which is a projection for the next year. This plan must be approved at several different levels of management. Once this is done we always run actuals for a given month to compare how are doing against the projections. Many organizations use a tiered funding process, where there are series of go/no-go decisions at each major stage of the program.

There are different types of BOMs depending on project and business needs, so your answer will draw directly from your own experience. If you've never worked with bills of materials, do not hesitate to say so; just be sure you convey that are familiar with them despite the lack of practical experience. – KG

17) Please explain Budget at Completion (BAC) vs. planned value (PV).

Answer: BAC is the entire budget allocated to a project; it is also used to calculate Estimate at Completion (EAC). Planned value represents the cost of the project for a given period of time. For example, the planned value for two months of a one-year project may be $50K, while the BAC is $300K ($50K x 6 two-month periods) for the entire project.

BAC and PV are used to track project performance. As a PM, you compare PV with earned value (EV) to decide whether the project is on schedule, or compare it with actual cost (AC) to determine if it is on budget.

18) What is a three-point estimate?

Answer: Three-point estimation is a technique used for the construction of an approximate probability distribution.

It represents the outcome of future events or activities based on limited information. It is used to calculate estimated duration based on best-case, most likely, and worst-case estimates.

Three-point estimates include the following parameters:

- P = Pessimistic estimate
- M = Most likely estimate
- O = Optimistic estimate

The estimated expected duration is calculated as = $(P+4M+O)/6$.

19) What is hammock?

Answer: Hammock is a summary activity that represents a group of related activities. Hammock is not a milestone; it is an activity that summarizes other activities.

20) What is resource histogram?

Answer: Resource histogram is a column chart that shows the number of resources assigned to a project over time. It helps in understanding long-term resource availability and workload.

21) As a PM, what sections would you include in the program plan?

Answer: The program plan is the overall reference by which the program will be measured for success throughout its duration. The program plan contains many elements and includes different documents. It formally expresses the organization's concept, vision, mission, and expected benefits from the program. It sets program-specific goals and objectives and gives authority for constituent sub-programs, projects, and related activities to be initiated.

22) How do you perform program cost budgeting?

Answer: Developing a program cost budget entails the compilation of all financial information, including income and payment schedules. This should be very detailed so that program's cost can be tracked as a part of the program budget baseline. After baselining, the baseline becomes the primary financial target against which program performance will be measured.

There are two important parts in program cost budgeting:

Program payment schedule: Schedule and milestones where funding is received by funding organization

Component schedule: Details when the contractors/vendors will be paid as per the contract provisions

23) What do you know about management reserve (MR)?

Answer: This term is used in cost management during estimation and budgeting. It is the portion of the contract budget that is withheld for management control purposes. The reserve is intended for unforeseen work that is within the scope of the project. However, special management authorization is required in order to use the MR.

24) What is WBS dictionary?

Answer: WBS dictionary is a document that provides detailed deliverables, activities, and scheduling information about each component in work breakdown structure (WBS). It also includes responsible organization, resources required (by skill level), cost estimates, basis of estimates, assumptions, contact information, etc.

25) What is resource breakdown structure (RBS)?

Answer: RBS lists all the resources (both human and non-human) required to execute the project. It includes people, equipment, materials, supplies, and any other direct or indirect item required.

26) How is apportioned effort used?

Answer: Apportioned effort is used for work with a direct supportive relationship to a discrete task. The value of the support task is determined based on earned value of the referenced base activity. This effort can include work such as quality assurance, inspection, testing activities, etc. It is generally estimated as a percentage of the referenced discrete work.

27) What are the different things that you consider before creating WBS?

Answer: As we know, WBS helps project managers and stakeholders communicate a clear vision of the end products and the process by which those products will be created. The following are things one must consider before creating WBS:

- Is the project charter defined and issued?
- Is the scope statement defined and issued?
- Have the team and project manager formulated a vision of the final product, services, results, etc.?
- What are the project's component parts?
- How do these pieces work together?
- Is the business objective defined?

- Have activities that are needed to support the deliverables been identified?
- Have deliverables, both interim and final, been identified?
- Are there any external sources needed to contribute to the project, and have they been identified?

28) What are the different relationship types in project scheduling? And what are different types of dependencies on the tasks in your project schedule?

Answer:

Relationships:

- Finish to Start
  - The successor cannot start before the predecessor has finished.
- Start to Start
  - The successor cannot start before the predecessor has started.
- Finish to Finish
  - The successor cannot finish before the predecessor has finished.

- Start to Finish
  - The successor cannot finish before the predecessor has started.

Dependencies:

- Mandatory
  - Inherent in the nature of the work; cannot be done any other way.
- Discretionary
  - Based on the preference of the team; can be changed if needed.
- External
  - Something outside the project impacts something internal to the project.
- Internal
  - Dependencies that are within the project team's control.

29) What are the two types of network diagrams?

Answer: Network diagrams address all four types of relationships between the activities. The two types are as follows:

- Precedence Diagramming Model (PDM) or Activity on Node (AON)
  - Boxes are used to show activities and arrows to show relationships.
- Arrow Diagramming Model (ADM) or Activity on Arrow (AOA)
  - Arrows represent activities and their directions indicate relationships.
  - Can only show Finish-Start relationships
  - May need to use dummy activities to show a dependency

30) What is rolling wave planning?

Answer: Rolling Wave Planning is a project planning technique that allows a project to be planned for as it unfolds. It is a process, not a tool.

Project planning is done in waves. Planning for the next phase is done while the execution of the previous phase is in progress. This is an iterative planning approach. As the project progresses, the risks, assumptions, and milestones originally identified become more defined and reliable. Rolling Wave Planning is used in instances where there is an extremely tight schedule or timeline to adhere to, and more thorough planning would have placed the schedule into an unacceptable negative schedule variance.

31) What are control accounts? What is the benefit of having control accounts in your project?

Answer: Control accounts are summary accounts supported by subsidiary-level accounts. In larger projects, it is difficult to manage costs at each individual activity level, so costs are managed at a level higher than the work package – in a control account.

Remember, the scope of a project is decomposed through a WBS. The lowest level deliverable in the WBS is called a work package, and a control account is above the work package. Control accounts allow you to track costs better than you can at work package level.

32) What is depreciation?

Answer:

In simple words, depreciation is the loss of value an asset over time. There are two forms of depreciation:

- Straight-line depreciation
  - The same amount of depreciation is provided for every year.
  - E.g. a car with a price tag of $10,000 and a useful life of 10 years is depreciated by $1,000 per year.
- Accelerated depreciation
  - The asset depreciates faster than the straight-line depreciation.
  - E.g. a car with a price tag of $10,000 depreciates $3,000 the first year, $1,500 the next year, $1,000 the third year, and so on.

33) What is human resource management (HRM)? As a PM, what HRM activities do you perform?

Answer: At a project level (as opposed to an organizational level), human resource management includes the processes that organize, manage, and lead the project team. The project team is composed of the people with assigned roles and responsibilities for completing the project.

The project management team is a subset of the project team; they are responsible for the project management and leadership activities such as initiating, planning, executing, monitoring and controlling, and closing the various project phases.

34) You are a project manager of the newly assigned project and you are explaining a complex algorithm to your team member. Suppose a team member is new. You explained all the details and asked if he has understood the same. He implies that he has understood it. You asked him to document the same. After going through the document, you found that the team member has not understood the algorithm. Who is responsible for this loss of time and how would you try to avoid it in future?

Answer: *This question is asked to evaluate your ability to take responsibility and blame. - KG*

As the PM, I am responsible for this loss of effort and inefficient use of time, since it is my responsibility to ensure my message is clear and concise and to confirm that the team member truly understands the message. In the communication model, it is the sender's responsibility to make the message clear, complete, and concise so that the recipient can receive it. The sender must also confirm that the recipient truly understands the message.

35) What is GERT?

Answer: GERT stands for Graphical Evaluation and Review Technique. It is a mathematical analysis technique which allows for probabilistic treatment of both network logic and estimation of activity duration. GERT also allows for conditional advancement, branching, and loopbacks.

36) If your project has slipped beyond its targeted finish date, what options could you employ to get back on track?

Answer: I could either Crash or Fast-Track the schedule. First and foremost, I would want to focus on the critical path tasks. I could assign additional resources to complete those tasks earlier, or perhaps employ some type of improved technology to complete things quicker. Either of these options would likely increase the overall cost of the project. This is known as Crashing.

Another option I could employ would be to examine the logic of the schedule, again focusing on the critical path tasks. I could change the logic of the project in order to do things in parallel. This approach generally comes with risks. For example, things will become more complex as there are now multiple tasks occurring at once. There is also a greater chance of rework using this technique. This is known as Fast-Tracking.

My final option, if the finish date was critical, would be to possibly cut some scope from the project in order to finish on time.

37) Name a few indicators that would show your project is in trouble and could fail.

Answer:

- Behind schedule

- Over budget
- Experiencing scope creep
- Sponsor is unsupportive
- Team is not following you
- No centralized communication
- People are unaware of critical things

8. Project Closing

1) Have you been PM on any projects that were failed? What do you feel was the main reason for failure, and how did you report this in your closure report?r

<u>Answer</u>: *This answer could be either yes or no. Ideally, you should avoid saying a project was failed. You can say in a diplomatic way, for example, that you were managing a project where the cost was overrun and the schedule slipped by 2 months. -KG*

<u>Example</u>: A platform migration project (e.g. Oracle to SAP) where you have vendor resources and their onboarding was delayed, approval for BOM got delayed, server deployment was delayed due to BOM approval, etc.

You can share your own experience as well. Make sure that you have valid reasons for each delay you mention which resulted in slippages.

Alternatively, you can say that you were involved in a failed project, not as a project manager, but in a previous role where you were one of the team members (in whatever capacity).

Some typical reasons projects fail are as follows:

- Incorrect requirements
- Following waterfall style methodology when agile was more suitable
- Catering to too many business users with conflicting versions of requirements and not being able to manage them
- Not having control over vendors and letting them mismanage the project
- Not having strong communication and control over the offshore or onsite development team and letting them make many assumptions in design
- Projecting very aggressive and unrealistic timelines to please management and not being able to follow through with it
- Incorrect assumptions during estimation
- A huge change in circumstances, like an internal or externally driven change in the project scope or resources

- Inadequate and inaccurate testing of the code before moving it to UAT

2) What is CSAT? Have you ever used this term in your projects?

Answer: CSAT is a customer satisfaction score, i.e. a measure of the customer's satisfaction with the services she received.

CSAT can vary from 0% to 100%.

Be prepared to discuss whether you've used CSAT in your own projects. – KG

3) Suppose you are approaching the closing phase of your project and a big change request comes in. You discuss this with the sponsor and the client and decide to implement it. At the same time, you agree to release a team member next week for another project. Now you cannot release her due to this change request. The other PM wanting to hire this team member is chasing

you. How will you deal with this situation?

Answer: This type of situation happens in projectized organizations. The situation mentioned in this question is expected in any projectized organization where resources working on a given project, which is approaching closure phase, are locked in for the next project by another PM.

If your project is going to extend due to a change request, you can communicate this to the other PM who is pressuring you to release the resource. (S)he would likely understand the situation and may not raise a question.

However, you can always loop in your superiors in case questions are raised by the other PM. Note that the project which is in progress (your project) would be given preference ahead of the project which has not yet begun, so you wouldn't have to worry too much about this.

4) At what point do you consider your project to be successful?

Answer: This is a basic question. Do not overanalyze it. A project is successful when the customer's needs and expectations are met or exceeded. Once you get the sign-off on the project deliverables that is when your project is successful. Note that there are other factors as well, such as whether you delivered on time and within the cost.

5) What is your definition of success, and how do you evaluate the success of the project?

Answer: *Stick to your basic definition of success. Everyone has his or her own definition of it. - KG*

Examples:

- Success is when I am performing well and satisfied with my position, knowing that my work is adding value to my company as well as to my overall life and the lives of others.
- I evaluate success based on outcomes. It's not always the path you take to achieve success that matters, but rather its quantifiable results.
- I evaluate success based not only on my work, but also on the work of my team. For me to be considered successful, the team needs to

achieve both our individual and overall team goals.

6) As a PM, in which phase of the project do you document lessons learned?

<u>Answer</u>: Lessons learned are documented during the closure phase. But as a proactive PM, you should document lessons learned as you learn them, and you should encourage your team to do the same.

9. Management Reporting

1) As a PM, you must provide weekly status reports to senior management. The report should be a single page/e-mail screen. What all will you include in the report?

Answer: I would include the following:

- Present status (an indicator - green, yellow or red),

- Highlights (e.g. milestones delivered, any feedback from the customer, cost performance index (CPI), schedule performance index (SPI), etc.)

- Other performance indicators (e.g. upcoming milestones, risks/issues and the corresponding mitigation plans for same, etc.)

The idea is to keep the above information to a one-page maximum, editing out portions that cause the information to go beyond a page.

2) You have been asked to share the EVM report of the project you are tracking in

MS project. How would you generate it? What does an EVM report tell about the project?

Answer: An Earned Value Management (EVM) report gives all the project indicators in terms of cost and schedule.

EVM helps measure the project's performance and its progress in an objective manner.

In MS project, you can simply go to "report" and generate an EVM report.

3) **You are presenting the project status during a project review meeting. You have just been asked to highlight any areas of concern. You have presented your project status as yellow. How would you quickly explain the yellow color status?**

Answer: Yellow color says your project is in 'attention' status. It indicates you are not on track to deliver the committed scope by the committed deadline with the committed resources/funding, but you have a plan to get back to green. The main difference between yellow and red is that in yellow status, you have a plan to get back to green, and in red status, you have no such plan.

4) What are different types of variances that you report in your project?

Answer: We generally report variance with respect to cost and schedule using CPI and SPI, respectively.

5) You are the project manager for a complex project, and you need to convey some very complex, detailed information to the project stakeholders. What would be the best method of communication for you?

Answer: Information that is complex and detailed is best conveyed in writing. Generally, verbal communication is used for follow-ups, answering simple questions, etc.

Written communication is the method of communication used for conveying important, complex, critical, sensitive information to the project stakeholders.

10. PM-Related Software Tools

1) Which project management tools have you used?

Answer: Give your best answer with all the tools you have used and have experience with. You may get other questions, such as how you'd rate yourself from 1-10 in these skills, or questions about how to use the tools.

While this answer will depend on your persona experience, some tools you'll likely mention are MS project, Clarity, Rally, Jira, Primavera, HP PPM, etc.

Of course, email and Excel are used on an ongoing basis. Most interviewers will look for Microsoft Project to be included in the answer. MS Project has something like a 75-80% market share for project management software on the desktop. If you understand how to work with MS Project, it is commonly accepted that you think like a project manager.

Additional points are generally given to individuals who have experience working with an Enterprise Project Management solution like Microsoft Project Server or Clarity.

2) Is it possible to have a separate calendar in MS project for each of your team members working on the project?

Answer: Yes, absolutely. For each resource on your project team, you can set up his or her own calendar.

3) What is resource leveling? How do you do it in MS project?

Answer: Resource leveling is a technique, widely used in the PM field, in which the start and end dates are adjusted based on the resource constraints. The goal of resource leveling is to balance the demand for resources and the available bandwidth (supply). In MS project, you can find a resource leveling option via Menu > Options > Resource leveling

4) What is the typical duration of a milestone in MS project?

Answer: The typical duration of a milestone in MS project is '0'.

5) **You are using Clarity for time reporting. Each member of your team must complete their timesheet in Clarity. How would you track your actual hours charged from the time entered in Clarity? Which report would be useful for you?**

Answer: You can generate a "Time by Task" report by going to Resource/Project manager time. You can then apply the filter against the investment ID (project code).

6) **What are the major components of Project Server?**

Answer: This answer should include the following: Microsoft Project, PWA, Project Sites, Project Center, Resource Center, Consolidated List of Tasks, Consolidated List of Issues and Risks, and a document repository.

7) **What are the benefits of working with Project Server?**

Answer: Enterprise insight into projects, enterprise resource pool combining efforts across all projects, time entry and/or task updates via the web, standard WBS templates, and project repository.

8) **Working in a Project Server environment, describe how you add resources to your project.**

Answer: You would add the resource from enterprise resource pool.

9) **Do you know the 3 variables within the scheduling formula of MS Project?**

Answer: Units x Duration = Work (or a similar formula using the same three fields, but solving for a different variable).

Knowing this answer is indicative of very sharp MS Project skills. - KG

10) **How would you go about finding Over-allocated resources on your team if you were working in a project server environment?**

Answer: The most common way would be to examine resources through Resource Center. You can see who is assigned to what, as well as their overall allocation. However, it is possible to change the setting in MS Project to see across all projects (that setting is available when you first launch MS Project).

11) Tell me how you feel about the automatic leveling feature of MS Project.

Answer: MS Project only knows how to delay tasks or split tasks. If you have over-allocated resources, it will inevitably extend the project finish date. It creates a worst-case scenario. In the real world, there are many ways to resolve over-allocations as opposed to simply delaying or splitting a task.

11. Application Development Management and DevOps

Project managers can be technical or non-technical. Most PM roles do not require hands-on knowledge of technology but expect a familiarity with the software development life cycle and the various software implementation activities at a concept level. The prior sections were geared toward project managers who fit into that category.

However, sometimes the PM also must double up as an application development manager. This can range from very technical where the PM also acts as the architectural advisor for the development team, to a less technical version where (s)he takes ownership of the build and release activities for implementation. The questions in this section revolve more around the build release and implementation activities. Technology architecture is excluded because it is a very case-specific subject and can be completely different based on the platform, tool, or programming language.

1) What were your primary responsibilities as an application development PM?

Answer:

- Working with the technology architect to ensure that the right architectural considerations are made
- Considering development escalations and resolving them
- Working on the release calendar and ensuring that all internal and external groups needed for successful release were aware of the expectation
- Overseeing production support and enhancement management for applications
- Overseeing all hardware and software requirements of the project
- Owning the entire ITSM (Information Technology Service Management) process for all the major and minor releases
- Ensuring that development best practices were followed by the team
- Ensuring completion of administrative tasks, such as managing details of team members,

static and dynamic scans related to application risk, access to integrated development environments, functional IDs, configuration management, etc.

- Ensuring correct details of the application are available in the application directory

2) What were some of the main shared services groups you would interact with as a part of your role?

Answer: Some groups that I had to interact with daily were:

Technology infrastructure: This group considers the software and hardware needs of the firm. If you want software licenses, space on a physical server, a share of a cloud server, or access to liquid infrastructure, this is the group you consult.

Operate: This group typically assists with any access to the servers. Usually, in large companies, there are strict restrictions on who can access production data and/or servers directly. The operate group acts as a layer to help you with any activity that requires server access, like getting data logs or usage logs for analysis, letting you know whether software processing or hardware capabilities have hit upper limits, or moving code from one environment to another during releases.

Development office: This shared group typically makes recommendations or mandates on the development best practices and/or the tools to use.

Shared services groups: Often peripheral or transient tasks, like software quality assurance, business analysis, process consulting, IT risk consulting, or data center of excellence, are not dedicated members of your team. They belong to centralized shared teams and are loaned to your project only on an as-needed basis. You need to interact with such shared service groups based on the demands of your projects.

All companies have some variation of the groups listed above, and typically all these groups also have some in-house applications that they use to provide service to different projects. A PM acting as the application development manager needs to be familiar with the groups and their respective applications. - KG

3) Can you describe the typical ITSM (I.T. Service Management) process you follow for your releases?

Answer:

- Typically, we create ITSM entries in an in-house system 2 weeks before the release. This entry includes a lot of detail on the features of the release, who is required, timing, etc.
- The plans written in the ITSMs must be reviewed in detail
- The various plans inside the ITSM must be approved by various parties.
  - E.g. implementation plans, roll back plans, results of static and dynamic application scans, UAT signoff emails, and other such evidence of completion
- Releases usually happen on Friday after business hours so that the application usage is not affected

4) Can you describe the typical enhancement management process you follow once your project is in BAU mode?

Answer: Once the initial rollout of the product is completed, I generally follow the following steps for enhancement management:

- Collect, compile, and prioritize the enhancement requests from during and after UAT
- Enter all requests in an enhancement management system, like JIRA, RALLY, etc.
- Hold sessions with the business and technology teams to discuss exact prioritization. Prioritization typically depends primarily on business urgency, availability of a workaround, ease of implementation, and resource availability
- The technology team bundles the enhancements using all of the above factors into releases (either sprint releases if it's Agile or regular ad hoc releases if methodology is not that well defined)
- Each release then goes through its development cycle and the product keeps getting upgraded

5) What kind of production support models are you familiar with?

Answer: Production support is a key activity after the initial launch. I have managed large support teams for many complex projects. Sometimes I am given a shared service team that is exclusively meant for production support, while other times we use members of the development team to manage support. On occasion, it is a mix of the two.

Typically, if it's a smaller project/product with a smaller user base and less criticality, it will suffice to have just a few members of the original development team managing support. This works because the developers are not only familiar with the code, but also know the business functionality very well.

However, for complex cross-functional and cross-organizational projects/products this is not adequate. We need a much greater division of labor for such critical products.

Usually, the level 1 support will be someone from the business side who is very familiar with the processes and also knows the product. Any issues the users encounter go to this group first. Level 2 support consists of production support professionals. Typically, I have the BA and other subject matter experts train the production support staff in nuances of the business functionality and the code structure. We also use systems like JIRA or Alacrity to automate the support process. Any items raised by the users that the level 1 team considers a production issue are handed over to the level 2 team via an entry into the production support system.

The level 2 team then analyzes the issue and classifies it as a training, performance, data, or functionality issue. Based on the type of issue, it is routed to the appropriate person in level 3 support. Level 3 is the actual developer who can resolve the issue and close the ticket.

The entire life cycle of an issue is tracked by the tool, and updates are provided to everyone involved. There are different resolution times permissible based on agreed SLAs of high, medium, and low items. Most production support tools come with full reporting capabilities, so I keep track of patterns of recurrence. This gives me an idea over time of where the problem areas lie and how things can be made more efficient by tackling the root cause.

6) What kind of development best practices do you implement in your projects?

Answer: There are several best practices supported by underlying tools and packages that are mandated by the development office; there are several others to which I personally request the architect adhere. I do not personally work on any of them, but am familiar with their usefulness and their function. Some of the tools and best practices I have adhered to in the past are:

- For requirements management, depending on the software development methodology we are following, we use different software applications.
  - o For Agile, I have found requirements management is easy with tools like Rally or JIRA.
  - o For waterfall style, good old Microsoft products like Word, Excel, and VISIO work perfectly fine.
  - o For very large projects, I recommend an end-to-end requirements management

tool like Enterprise Architect or Requisite Pro.

- o Additionally, iGrafx is good for process models, Erwin works well for data modeling, and wireframing tools like Axure are a must-have for business analysts
- When it comes to coding, the first thing is to have a good version control application like apache subversion (SVN)
- You should also have code review tools like Crucible, Google Gerrit or GitHub code comments, etc.
- Constant code scans are also required for static and dynamic scans. Products like Black Duck are useful for open source software
- Jenkins is a good tool for continuous integration
- The tool of choice for build automation is Apache-Maven

7) Why do you think we need DevOps?

Answer:

The ultimate objective of all I.T. service providers, regardless of whether they are internal or external providers, is customer satisfaction. DevOps helps achieve that end goal in the following ways:

- Reduces failure in new releases
- Ensures better frequency of deployment
- Facilitates reduced recovery time if failure does happen

8) Is DevOps the same as Agile??

Answer:

No.

Agile is an overall software development methodology. It will provide guidelines on all aspects of development from requirements management to production release. It has nothing to do with the technical aspect of build and release or deployment.

DevOps is specifically a concept which deals with integrating the functions of the development team and the operate team during the build and deployment and release management of code.

9) Can you provide a quick overview of the build and deploy process?

Answer:

While this may vary from organization to organization, a generic example is:

- Developers write code and it is managed by Version Control System tools like Git SVN.
- Any changes made in the code must be committed to this repository.
- A continuous integration tool like Jenkins pulls this code from the repository using the Git plugin and builds it using build automation tools like Ant or Maven.
- Configuration management tools like Puppet deploy code on the testing environment.
- Continuous integration tools like Jenkins release the code on the test environment.
- Test automation tools like Selenium do the automated testing.
- After testing, Jenkins sends it for deployment on the production server.
- Post-deployment code is continuously monitored by tools like Nagios.

10) Compare GIT vs. SVN.

Answer:

GIT is a Distributed Version Control system (DVCS). It does not depend on a code repository on a single central server. Instead, each developer has their own copy on a local machine and every team member is connected to each other via cloud. There is no worry of server outages. When any developer commits changes, others can see it via 'remote repository'.

Subversion (SVN), on the other hand, is centralized. There is one central server and copies of code are not stored in individual machines. One must connect to this server via the internet in order to work on it.

11) What steps do you take to make continuous integration easier?

Answer:

- Ensure discipline in maintaining a code repository and automating the build process
- Automate the build

- Make sure the build is self-testing
- Ensure that all developers commit to the baseline daily
- Make the latest deliverables and results of the latest build accessible
- Automate deployment

12. Agile Project Management

This section will cover some real-life practical questions about managing Agile projects. This is not an Agile training, so we assume that you are well-versed with most of the basic concepts of Agile SDLC. We build on that assumption and elaborate on questions that speak to different aspects of an agile implementation.

1) **Have you ever been involved in a major agile transformation from waterfall? Describe your experience.**

Answer: My latest project started off as waterfall, but the company decided to adopt Agile in the middle of it and for all projects going forward.

Since the project started as waterfall, we spent a lot of time documenting the details around requirements. We had a full suite of documentation including BRD, FRD, tech design, etc. We also had lots of details like process models, data models, and functional and non-functional requirements in the FRD.

The project was developed on-time and everything seemed to be on track. There were some issues with too many bugs found during QA, but it was easily overcome. When we moved the product to UAT we were very confident that we had completed everything successfully and were already patting ourselves on the back. Little did we know that a huge surprise awaited us. This was a cross-organizational application, so a central team had signed off on requirements. The actual users of the system had only taken a cursory look at the documents. Additionally, documents never do the justice that a real product can. Hence the users started giving actual feedback only after we provided them the UAT link. The result was a disaster.

Change after change was requested, and many fundamental things had to be rewritten. This resulted in a lot of wasted time and the project got delayed. By this time, the firm was also mandating Agile practice for all major projects. We thought this was a good opportunity to jump on the Agile bandwagon. In hindsight, we should have adopted Agile for our project from the beginning. We decided to do it for phase two.

It was a culture change not only for I.T. but also for the business side. I took on the role of a scrum master and the BAs assumed the product owner role. The first thing we did was create a proper product backlog based on the use cases that we had documented in the first phase. These epics and user stories were uploaded into Rally, where we now maintain them.

The next step was to have an iteration zero where we went over high-level requirements of what was needed in phase 2. We did have some basic documentation - enough to get started. Agile does not mean NO documentation, it merely means MINIMUM documentation.

Based on our iteration zero discussions, we started the sprint planning. We decided that 4-week sprints work best for us with 1 week of requirement fine tuning, 2 weeks of development, and 1 week of testing each sprint.

Instead of long, verbose FRDs, we now maintain process models in iGrafx. The process models also contain details of the business rules. One of the BAs became a UX consultant. We try to have mock screens in Axure so that requirements are modeled visually and we can react quickly to changes.

I had to change the way that I capture project progress. I still provide the standard weekly RAG reporting, monthly budget reports, and other management reports, but all I care about for the sprints are the burn up and burn down charts. I have formatted the data in a particular way to get this information, and it makes it easy to follow and incredibly useful.

We do a telephonic daily standup, as many team members are offshore, but it works well for us.

All-in-all, Agile has worked very well for us as we are more adaptive to change and have faster error-free deliveries. True, it does not lend itself to pure technology endeavors like tech refresh, server upgrades, software upgrades, and pure data migration projects. However, it has worked very well for regular projects, especially where business user interaction is involved.

2) Typically, context diagrams provide a context for the application's ecosystem in Waterfall. Do we need tools like context diagrams or state transition diagrams in Agile? If not, then how do developers know these details? For example, I'm working on a process flow project. This is an approval process flow where an initiative goes from creation state to fully approved state. There are many states in between, and there is value in knowing what trigger moves an initiative from one state to the next. How would I have shown this in Agile if there was no documentation?

Answer: Scrum framework does not "ban" documentation, it just states that working software is more important. That said, if the Scrum Team sees value in building a context diagram, they should do so. It can be an ongoing effort, and there can be multiple user stories for it in separate sprints. The idea behind Scrum and Agile is to focus on working software immediately. In waterfall development, we would start actual software development without having multiple artifacts first (e.g. requirements doc, architecture doc, use cases etc.). Scrum does not "ban" any of these artifacts if the Scrum Team and stakeholders see value in having them. Scrum simply states that development can start without having all these documents prepared. Indeed, for smaller projects (e.g. mobile apps, websites) teams usually do not produce all the documentation required for larger, enterprise systems. Once again, it is all a matter of planning and cost-benefit ratio.

3) **How exactly is wireframing done in Agile? Sometimes wireframes are all or nothing. Unless I have a holistic picture of how the system is going to work, it's very difficult for me to create it piece-by-piece. In Agile, however, there won't be time to create the entire wireframe. What then is the approach in Agile?**

Answer: The main difference between Agile and Waterfall, in this case, would be that in Waterfall we would spend 6 months wireframing the product and defining every single functionality and use case, and wouldn't start with development until the whole wireframe was done. In Agile, we would spend the first sprint or two working on the prototype that is the basic conceptualization of the product.

For example, let's say we were building an e-commerce application. We would start with a basic wireframe that will reflect what screens we think our application will have for each of the user roles we want.

Example:

Interface that end users will see:

- Landing page
- List of products page
- Single product page
- Shopping cart
- Payment process

First, we would do a low-fidelity prototype that would not go into details of what each screen would contain.

After finishing general wireframe, we would focus on each screen at the time and work toward a high-fidelity prototype. If we had the luxury of doing user testing or discussing our prototype with the client, we would iterate and change our design to best fit user/client needs before starting development.

This would minimize the chance that we are building something completely wrong, and is a basic principle of the Agile development – getting feedback and being on the right track. We would not predict every possible use case, but at this point, the client would have a pretty good idea as to what our application will look like and what will be the most important features. The main takeaway here is that there will be some trial and error, but that is the beauty of Scrum and Agile. Since we are working in short iterations (i.e. sprints), we are able to rapidly respond to changes in demands.

4) **In waterfall, the data models are critical to success. The developer will never be able to create the correct product unless I provide a detailed conceptual data model which specifies the attributes of each data element on the UI and on the backend. Additionally, if they are migrating data**

from an older system to a newer system they will absolutely need the mapping. However, I have never heard of detailed work being done on the data side in Agile.

How are requirements around data captured in Agile? Please explain with examples.

Answer: In Agile, the main difference is that you are always (first) thinking from the user perspective. In this case, you would create a user story describing what the user can accomplish, and then you would add acceptance criteria that can include details regarding the data model.

Since Scrum Teams are independent, there is no separate architecture team or team member assigned to architecture. Everything is decided within the Scrum Team.

Most importantly, things change. Scrum Team members have a lot more autonomy, and the team is responsible for all results.

If the Product owner sees value in describing a data model within a user story/acceptance criteria, then so be it.

In the case of data migration, we can:

- have an epic called "Migration" where we will describe everything that needs to be migrated, or

- We can create multiple user stories that will follow the development of functionalities that will depend on certain data being migrated.

5) How would you capture non-functional requirements in Agile?

Answer: Scrum Teams have a set of rules/artifacts that are applicable to every item/JIRA ticket the Scrum team delivers. This is called "Definition of Done" (DoD) and is considered a part of every single artifact/feature/item that Scrum Teams deliver.

Initial "DoD" is usually developed in the first sprint (or Sprint 0 if the team needs to have it). "DoD" evolves and expands as Scrum Teams work more and more together and add stricter quality standards.

All non-functional requirements need to be a part of the DoD criteria.

6) How do you capture the production support process and the enhancement request process in Agile style development?

Answer: When doing Sprint Planning, teams usually set aside a certain amount of capacity for unexpected production issues, support, etc. Teams use various techniques when estimating work (story points, working hours, etc.). What I typically do with my teams is plan for a 13-point "Sustainment & Maintenance" JIRA user story where team members capture all these urgent tasks, as well as other tasks that are not part of other sprint work. The important thing is that we allocate time for this.

7) In Agile, what does one do in cases of data-driven projects, infrastructure projects, legacy modernization projects, or tech refresh projects? How do you have user stories in these areas?

Answer: Scrum is not a silver bullet. For example, even support teams that want to practice Agile usually go with Kanban instead of Scrum. Every project has its specifics, and Scrum is not an ideal solution for every type of project. One must think through carefully on the intended objectives and the capacity to adapt to change before deciding to go for SCRUM-based SDLC.

8) **What happens when you realize in the middle of a sprint that you cannot deliver? Do you call off the sprint or do you deliver regardless? Give detailed examples.**

Answer: This is a common question, and the first problem I see is with the wording "cannot deliver". Since Scrum is all about responding to change and delivering work in chunks, sprints should always have a Sprint Goal. Sprint Goal is defined during the Sprint Planning and usually represents the main features (i.e. the most important items that will come out of that sprint). That said, these items are usually worked on first because they need to be delivered for the sprint work to be demoed and the sprint to be considered successful. Ideally, you should not have make-or-break features (i.e. a build should be deliverable with the features that are working). If there is a high-risk feature that we are unsure will fit in a single sprint, we usually start working on it on a separate branch and merge it only when we feel comfortable.

The Product Owner has the authority to cancel sprints if they no longer make sense (i.e. if the circumstances have changed so much that finishing the sprint as it was planned just doesn't bring any value).

In worst-case scenarios where the team estimate and commitment were so off that you have nothing to show, the Product Owner needs to go before the stakeholders and call that particular sprint a failure.

9) How exactly is testing planned and executed in Agile? Without adequate test documentation, how do you populate test cases into ALM? And if it cannot be in a tool like ALM, how you do ensure adequate coverage?

Answer: ALM test cases can be a part of the Scrum Team's Definition of Done (i.e. team members would write and maintain them). In larger-scale projects, you will need some way to track test coverage. In smaller projects, automated test scripts are usually what gives you an idea of system coverage.

Testing/QA is an integral part of every user story/feature. A feature is not delivered until testing is done on it. If the acceptance criteria and/or DoD also requires test cases in a test case management tool - so be it. Once again, Agile enables us to respond to change. Agile doesn't see value in writing every possible test case before we have a piece of working software because the assumption is that the software will change and evolve as the user and/or stakeholder needs it to evolve.

10) What all are the things that you should cover in iteration 0? How long does iteration 0 typically last?

Answer: Iteration 0 or sprint 0 lasts one sprint (sprint length is usually 1-4 weeks, 2 weeks being most common). Sprint 0 is usually used by teams that haven't worked together before to set up some infrastructure (code repository, hardware, initial Definition of Done, etc.). It is called sprint 0 since teams do not usually deliver working software out of this iteration.

11) **How do you decide what is a minimum viable product? What if the product is all-or-nothing, like regulatory applications where you cannot have half of a regulation fulfilled?**

Answer: The Product Owner is responsible for optimizing the value of the work that the Scrum Team does. That said, he or she steers the team toward the MVP and decides what the MVP is. For regulatory applications, Scrum is probably not the best method to use.

While you can make Scrum work for these projects, they have some characteristics that are just not natural to Scrum (e.g. very strict deadlines, documentation and project scope needs to be agreed in advance, etc.).

12) **In Agile projects, how do you decide when an implementation is over and when the project is in BAU mode?**

Where does the project end and enhancement request begin?

Answer: At the end of every sprint, the Product Owner decides if the build should be deployed to Production. The team is responsible for making a Potentially Shippable Increment, but the Product Owner decides if and when to release it to Production.

At the end of the day, it depends on the type of project, users, and other teams (e.g. sales, marketing, etc.). For example, if you are building a B2C product and have an assumption you want to validate, you will go to production very early (as soon as possible). At other times, you want to build a complete solution and then release it to users.

Even though you are doing the core software development in a new framework (Scrum), there are still other factors and marketplace rules for releasing products that influence decisions like this one.

13. People Management and Leadership

1) Have you directly managed people? If so, what were your main objectives?

Answer: Yes, I have managed people directly. My team sizes have been anywhere from 5 to 15 (you can state whatever your team sizes were but typically for a mid-level PM it's between 5-15). Some of my responsibilities/objectives were:

- Serve at the face of the organization and its culture
- Communicate everything from corporate standards to expected compliance, approvals for various needs, timesheets, administrative items, organization change, and news
- Create a friendly environment where team can work well together and negotiate internal conflicts
- Recognition of high-performing individuals and helping anyone that is struggling to achieve full potential
- Career management of direct reports

- One-off activities like hiring, new joiners, and people leaving the firm

At the end of the day, leadership is all about leading oneself, leading people, and the business you represent. There must be a mental switch where you focus more on the success of your team and understand that it relates to your success. That's a transition from thinking like an individual contributor.

2) What are the various leadership styles that you are familiar with? What are the pros and cons of each style you have observed?

Answer: There are many leadership studies that classify leadership into distinctive styles. However, the classification that appealed to me was as follows:

Persuading leader: This style persuades people using compelling sales pitches. They are creative, high energy, passionate risk-takers. However, they get bored easily and may become overly emotional under stress.

Counseling leader: This style is more empathetic and uses coaching as a means of leadership. They are casual and approachable, which keeps the team at ease. However, sometimes they are very consensus driven and are unable to put their foot down when they should.

Directing leader: This style is more hands-on, independent, and results-oriented. However, sometimes they can be so controlling and focused on results that they overlook the people side.

Analyzing leader: This leadership style uses a lot of data and analysis to drive decisions. They are logical, organized, and detailed. On the flip side, they can be risk averse and prefer analysis over action in difficult situations.

3) What is your mentoring style for people that report to you?

<u>Answer:</u> There are certain things that I always ensure for my direct reports:

- If it's a new member, I take special care to ensure that all available and required training material is provided to him/her and they are up to speed with a minimal learning curve.

- I coach people to not lose sight of the big picture even when they are working on details.

- At the very onset, I establish a recurring one-on-one meeting so that any discussion related to deliverables, performance, questions, or concerns can be addressed in real time and not in a reactive manner.

- I also make sure that I understand the person's aspirations and career needs so that (s)he can be steered in that direction and assisted as required.

- I prefer complete delegation of tasks and teaching people to own their deliverables, and I typically only get involved as necessary. Micro management is never beneficial to anyone in the long run.

4) What is your experience with organization change management?

Answer: Change is the only constant in life, and in the workplace, it can be of many types. Organization change can be in terms of a reorganization, new management, new processes, or a new project. I can talk at length about each type of change I've experienced and my reactions as a project manager, but an extrapolation of the common elements is as follows:

Engage all stakeholders: Sometimes it is convenient to discuss impactful changes to only a limited circle of people that we are personally comfortable with. However, this is detrimental as no large change is ever possible without involvement and support of everyone involved. Even if there is initial pain, everyone must feel it's for the larger long term good or else the change will fail.

Describe the change as a benefit: People do not react well if any large change comes as a mandate. Instead, it should be personalized and explained as to why it is a benefit for the individual and how a lot of thought was put behind it.

Constantly communicate: A lot of times people forget this basic step. A huge change is always an anxious period for everyone. It is essential to regularly provide updates, vision, expectations, and any other communication that puts people's minds at ease.

Do not let legacy systems/processes make the decision for you: A change is required because we are going to move to a different style of working. This is why it is important to not be attached to the previous way and make decisions on how that worked. Disassociation from the legacy system and taking a fresh look at things is essential.

5) What is delegation vs. dumping, and how do you ensure effective delegation?

<u>Answer</u>: Delegation is the key skill required by any people manager. It's the process of assigning tasks strategically with a view of getting a good deliverable and grooming employees to own things. Dumping is merely giving away tasks that you do not like to others without any explanation.

In delegation, you explain the benefit, importance, expected quality, and the timelines for a task and expect the person to own it completely. The manager is judged by the results achieved by delegation and not by which tasks (s)he delegates to whom.

I use a mix of the employee's competence and commitment to a particular task to ensure effective delegation. High competence and high commitment need little supervision. A person with high commitment but low competence for that task needs step-by-step instructions. People with low competence and low commitment need a lot of hand-holding. This is one area where micromanagement is occasionally required until either the competence or commitment level is raised. Employees should not be permitted to stay for too long in this state because it can harm the ultimate deliverable and also spoil the morale of the team.

6) How do you set objectives with your direct reports so that the performance review goes smoothly?

Answer: We typically do quarterly performance reviews with a final annual review that happens at the end of the year. This is one of the most important things about being a manager, as the compensation and career progression of your employees depends on this.

Around January of every year, we enter objectives in the performance management system. I make sure that the employee objectives are **S**pecific, **M**easurable, **A**greed upon, **R**ealistic, and **T**ime-based. This is referred to as **SMART** objective setting.

Throughout the year, I have at least a weekly one-on-one with my direct reports where they can discuss any topic around work deliverables and feedback. This ensures that they are getting constant and honest feedback throughout the year and the quarterly reviews do not come as a surprise. Additionally, I request that any positive or negative review be documented (like storing emails, etc.) so that it does not end up becoming one person's word against the other.

Giving positive feedback is essential, but relatively easy. It is the negative feedback that needs a lot of tact and empathy. If delivered incorrectly, it can make the person defensive, and that does not serve anyone's purpose.

One must first explain the context, the action taken by the individual, and the result of taking the action. Instead of berating or demeaning the individual, one should then provide positive reinforcement by saying what the alternative action is and how that would have had a different result. This makes it more of a constructive feedback rather than personal indictment.

7) What are some ways you have motivated your employees in the past?

Answer: Keeping the employees motivated to do the job is one of the key aspects of leadership. There is a misconception that compensation is the only motivator. It's true that it is a big motivator, but not the only one. Additionally, most employees assume that as a manager you have power over everything like compensation, policies, promotions, etc. That is not the case either. I consider a mix of things as motivators like compensation, company policy, work environment, team dynamics, recognition, ability to work on interesting projects and make a difference, etc. As a leader, I have a knack for understanding my team's mental make-up and gauging who is motivated by what. To the greatest extent possible, I use a mix of these and tailor make the tasks for each person to ensure that they are motivated. Additionally, I am very honest in explaining why certain things are not in my control and how I did my best using factors that were. This ensures that my team is not bitter even if sometimes they do not get what they want.

8) What are some ways in which a manager can subconsciously favor one employee over the other, and how can it be avoided?

Answer: There are some subconscious behaviors that we may not realize right away, but can be noticed by other people; examples include:

- Consistently inviting only some people for formal or informal meetings
- Giving some individuals more information than the others
- Interrupting some people and criticizing them in public
- Responding to smooth talkers rather than focusing on substance and outcome

- Not rotating meetings to accommodate individuals in offshore locations
- Relying on first impressions rather than getting to know people based on skills, achievement, and potential.

All of us are guilty of having done the above, as they are only human tendencies. However, as a manager, it is our responsibility to constantly monitor ourselves and stop it whenever we catch ourselves doing the above.

9) Have you managed virtual teams? If yes, what are some ways to ensure good communication?

Answer: Yes, I have managed team members that work from home in a secondary location within the US or in offshore locations. It is different from having a team in front of you. Unless one is careful it is easy to slip off the radar and ignore the virtual team members, and they may start feeling like they have a secondary status. This should always be avoided as virtual team members are as much of an integral part of your team as in-person team members.

Some things that have helped me manage communications with virtual team members better are:

- Understand their timing preference and make sure that there are regular touchpoints where they are involved
- Use technology like telepresence or video conference to maintain a personal connection as much as possible
- Be mindful of cultural and time zone differences

10) Have you managed in a matrix situation where the people do not directly report to you?

Answer: Yes, I have frequently led teams that did not directly report to me. This happens when I inherit people from shared resources groups or if it's an offshore team that has a local manager. There is a certain degree of loss of control because of that, but it can be managed. It is essential in such cases to have regular one-on-one meetings with the person's manager so that constant feedback is provided. Additionally, a coaching or mentoring style of leadership should be followed as it's essential to gain the respect of the team members that do not directly report to you.

11) Have you ever fired anyone? When would you take such a step?

Answer: Yes, unfortunately, there have been occasions in the past when I had to let go of people. There can be three main reasons for this:

- Budget cuts
- Underperformance
- Indiscipline or breach of basic policy

One must be extremely sensitive in any of these cases as it's a major upheaval in the life of the person. For budget cuts, I typically explain to the person how it was absolutely not their performance because of which this step needs to be taken. And explain how unfortunately sometimes it's a financial decision.

Underperformance has several reasons ranging from general lack of discipline to personality clashes, incompetence in the job, not having skills required for the job, lack of commitment, or personal problems. In such situations, I give honest feedback, hand-holding, and coaching to see if the situation can be remedied. I try to be as specific as possible with the feedback so that the person has a genuine chance to improve. Additionally, if there appears to be a personal reason, I provide a lot of latitude to the person to help them sort it out but still make it clear that it should not affect their quality of work. If the situation is because of a skill set mismatch I would try to coach the person out of the job into a different profile. If none of this works then the only way out which is sometimes best for all parties is to let the person go.

For serious issues like severe indiscipline, breach of security, or disregard for basic business ethics, the only way out is making a fast, irreversible decision. I make every effort to let people know in the very beginning about compliance with basic policies and if this red line is crossed then the only option is to let the person go with immediate effect.

14. Dissecting Projects on Your Résumé

Your interview and the answers that you provide are closely related to your résumé. Your résumé is the single most critical aspect of getting a foot in the door. Additionally, remember that most interviews are never longer than 1 hour per person, so there is only enough time to focus on your résumé and find out whether you are a good fit.

That being said, a lot of the answers that we have provided in this book *must be customized by you* based on the projects that you have listed on your résumé. However, before you customize the answers, you need to have a visceral understanding of the projects listed on your résumé. Hence, we would advise you to make 'project flash cards' for at least the projects spanning the last 5 years on your résumé.

A project flash card lists out the most important business and technology summary points about a given project and your role in it. This serves as a good cheat sheet for you to get familiar with your talking points.

Most interviews start with the interviewer asking you to give an elevator talk on some of your recent projects. It is often said that the first five minutes are when most of the decisions are made. The rest of the interview is usually spent validating the decision made from that first impression. It is thus critical for you to put your best foot forward when you provide the project overview.

We have created a sample 'project flash card' for a project which will help you to create your own. The flashcard can be found on the next page.

What does the company do? Fannie Mae is the leading source of residential mortgage credit in the U.S. secondary market; it is supporting today's economic recovery and helping to build a sustainable housing system.

What was the business problem? Fannie Mae was handling and restructuring millions of dollars' worth of loans each minute but the systems they used were homemade excel reporting tools. This was initially managed by a huge team of loan processing analysts who used to manually update every single loan details and restructure them which resulted in inefficiencies mainly slow processing time, which was the result of the loan processing team updating and restructuring loans, periodic reporting since the team reported every month end and inaccuracies due to manual reporting.

What was the objective of your project? The leadership wanted us to build an OBIEE system that would:

Automate the process of restructuring delinquent loans to reduce the number of foreclosures that we were going through and align the process with regulatory standards like HUD Hamp guidelines.

Report key mortgage metrics on a constant daily basis like mortgage installments, balance, modified interest rate and term of the loan, and LPI dates. This system offered significant benefits like automation of millions of mortgage reporting and restructuring data, reducing processing time, and improving data accuracy.

What were the key challenges? The main challenge was lack of time. There had been several delays in the early part of the project which resulted in a very compressed time frame for quality assurance to be completed. The second challenge was that the requirements document was incomplete, as the BA had changed in the middle of the project, and continuity in the documents was an issue. Finally, there were a lot of data-related details that resulted in intense manual testing.

What results did the project achieve? The project went live in 18 months. We achieved great results. The transition to an Oracle-based system reduced processing time by 50%. For example, before the system went live, it would take 10 team members to update the Excel reporting every 24 hours. After transition, the Oracle interface automatically updates reports every 12 hours without human intervention. The system also improved accuracy by 60%.

15. In Conclusion

As you've learned throughout this text, you need to build a strong case that you are the best fit for the job. In doing so, you need to ensure that you:

- Link key points in your résumé to the job being offered;
- Avoid negativity of any kind, such as talking bad about a past employer, manager, or even yourself;
- Breathe life into the interview by using examples from your experience, and prove that you have the right attitude and team spirit; and
- Drive the interview to your strong points, avoiding discussion concerning your weaker areas.

Best of luck going out and getting the job you so deserve. We are here to help, so please feel free to give us a call or send us an email at info@kuebikoglobal.com. In addition to online training, we also offer sample résumé and mock interview packages.

Note to reader: We would love to hear your feedback. Please send your comments, billing inquiries, and suggestions for future updates to info@kuebikoglobal.com.

Sign up to receive our exclusive introductory gift ($15 value) by sending an email to info@kuebikoglobal.com. We will send you a powerful, highly-customized, 200-slide PPT toolkit that contains detailed slides for any kind of management preparation. Using this, you will never have to work on a PowerPoint slide from scratch again. Plus, you will never miss out on new tutorials, tips, and updates!

Kuebiko Global provides innovative online training and career support programs in a variety of information technology management areas and associated business operations. We specialize in providing practical real-world knowledge and skills that are required for success in the modern IT industry. Our experienced professionals take inspiration from "Kuebiko," the Japanese god of wisdom.

We offer training and consulting, coupled with industry domain knowledge, in various areas of the techno-functional space, including business systems analysis, project management, quality assurance, technology recruitment, and niche software packages. Our training services are ideal for working professionals looking to diversify their skill sets, college students seeking to start their careers and companies looking for a training partner.

Thank you,
Kuebiko Global